ON GOD AND TRAUMA

Hope for Moral Injury and Survivor Guilt

Lt Col David F. Tharp, PsyD., M. Div.

This is a work of non-fiction. All the events in this book really happened. However, the opinions and interpretations expressed in this book are mine alone and do not reflect those of anyone else or of any of the individuals with whom I served. They also do not necessarily reflect the official policy or position of the United States Air Force, Department of Defense, the Department of Veterans Affairs, the United States Government, Texas A&M University, Baylor University, Project Healing Heroes, and/or CombatPTSD.org. These events occurred almost a decade ago, so the conversations in this book are recounted according to the best abilities of my memory. Some details in the book have been changed to respect patient confidentiality. The story, all names, characters, and incidents portrayed in this book are fictitious except for the permissions that have been granted for use. No identification with actual persons, places, buildings, and products is intended or should be inferred. The US Air Force Academy Public Affairs Officer reviewed the manuscript to ensure it did not compromise the security of our military and approved it for publication.

All pictures in this book are in the public domain unless otherwise noted. If there is erroneous credit, please contact the authors, and we will make appropriate changes in future editions.

If you or someone you know is experiencing thoughts of suicide, please contact 911 immediately or the suicide hotline at 1-800-273-8255. To find a suicide helpline outside the US, visit the International Association for Suicide Prevention website or Suicide.org. If you or someone you know is experiencing post-traumatic stress (disorder) or other issues, and are a veteran, contact the Department of Veterans Affairs at 1-800-827-1000. All other symptoms that require immediate attention, please contact 911.

This book is not intended to replace therapy in any way. There is no patient-therapist or client-therapist relationship intended or unintended by the use of the materials in this book. We strongly encourage you to reach out to a mental health provider and share with them your intent to get healthy and regain your life.

Lt Col David F. Tharp, PsyD, M. Div.
Visit the Project Healing Heroes website at www.ProjectHealingHeroes.org.
Printed in the United States of America

ISBN - 9781091157019

PREFACE

Is This Book for Me?

Who should read this book? At <u>Project Healing Heroes</u>, we truly believe that anyone can find hope and healing, wherever they are in life, even when it comes to very different views and opinions. One reader may be agnostic, while another, deeply religious. That being said, we have found some common themes that make a direct impact on how well people do after trauma, one of them being a close relationship with someone they trust. It takes a lot to trust someone in this world. And when we find someone who is trustworthy, it can make for a healthy, resilient relationship. Sometimes, we need to be vulnerable, but only to the right people. You know them - the people in your life that you can trust. You can probably count them on one hand, or maybe even one finger, but hopefully, you have someone who measures up. If you could trust someone implicitly with your life, who comes to mind?

Hopefully, it is someone with whom you can be honest and vulnerable, someone with whom you can share your deepest fears, insecurities and questions. We all have them. Every one of us. If this book does nothing else, hopefully, it will encourage you to evaluate who you can turn to in times of need. And not just hope they reach out to you, but you reach out to them. It truly takes courage to ask for help. And warriors know a thing or two about courage!

We all seek relationships in various places. For the agnostic, it may mean turning to a trusted friend. For the deeply religious, it may be turning to God and others.

As a formula for success: Relationships + Resources = Resiliency

How to Read This Book

I have two recommendations when it comes to the material in this book.

First, be willing to see things from different perspectives. Clarity will come in the following chapters, but for now, the analogy of a camera is simple and precise. *The lens by which you see yourself, others and the world has been altered by war.* Let that sink in for a moment. *The lens by which you see yourself, others and the world has been changed.* It has changed who you are, the choices you make, and the course of your life. You are no longer the same person you once were. At your core, you know that to be true. So how do we take back our life? In our analogy, we must examine each choice we make. What you do with aperture, focus, speed, balance, even the filters and lens you use, truly matters. Each setting changes the picture - your picture, your life.

At the end of this paragraph, look up and stop reading for a moment. Stop and take a snapshot of your life and what it has become. Note your surroundings, the people in your life, the issues you are facing and how you interpret them. Are they out of focus, overexposed, blurry? Every decision you make directly impacts the quality and outcome of your life. Turn your head, and scan with your eyes from left to right that which is in front of you. Then contemplate what is there...and not there.

For Christmas, I received a very expensive gift: a Panasonic Lumix GH5 DSLR camera with an Atomos Shogun Inferno that records 4K video in ProRes 422 at 10 bits per second. Needless to say, the setup captures incredibly vivid pictures and video. I spent considerable time learning about its capabilities, working with each function and understanding the intricacies of photography. And then it was time. Time to test it out. I was meticulous in getting everything ready. Hauling the tripod, camera and external recording equipment isn't easy, but worth it. I found the perfect location. After accomplishing the physical setup, I then switched to lens selection, white balance, aperture settings, focus points, even using histographs and zebra settings. I was excited to take video of my son playing basketball. I say "was" because the last thing that went through my mind was to grab an extra battery. After spending my entire time setting up the camera, I was focused on what I thought was important. In trying to get everything perfect, I had exhausted my resources. My camera battery was nearly spent. I had done everything I thought was right. Unfortunately, in making sure everything was nearly perfect, I had expended almost all of the batteries' energy. My battery life was in the red, and there was no spare. I had spent too much time focusing on what I thought was important.

Life is sometimes like that. We can spend enormous amounts of energy on things that we believe are important. And seeing it only from our perspective, we miss the mark. Most often, it involves relationships.

Have you spent yourself to the point there isn't much left? Do the things you have seen and dream about keep you up at night? Are you depleted? Are you exhausted with life beyond what you ever thought or imagined? There is hope, and it is my intent to unveil ideas, concepts and a new perspective that will free you from the tyranny of your mind. In so doing, I hope to restore your energy and give you a new mission and purpose in life.

Second, understand that we all have blind spots. There are situations, circumstances, issues, etc., that we simply cannot see. Others in our life may see them and wish to bring them to our attention, but only if we are open and willing to listen. It is a risk on their part and yours. You probably know people who are unwilling to heed advice, even when it's in their own best interest. We call them "hardheaded." Instead, I encourage you to be malleable, willing to be moldable, teachable, and open to something different. Be open to the process. In my family, we call it being FAT: Faithful, Available and Teachable. Are you FAT?

Personal Convictions

When it comes to issues of religion and spirituality, the United States was heavily influenced by Judeo-Christian beliefs and values, many of which continue today. That being said, we are also a very kind, generous and inclusive nation, one in which we fight for the freedoms of everyone. We even fight for values and beliefs that we may not even espouse. That is the true definition of inclusivity!

We continue that tradition at Project Healing Heroes. We do not believe we have all the answers or even attempt to solve all of the world's faith tradition questions. What we do is speak from the tradition we are most familiar with, trained in and believe. We strongly encourage those of other faith traditions to seek out their spiritual leaders and incorporate their spiritual beliefs to help them resolve issues of moral injury and survivor guilt. We would like to include guest writers to participate with us as we share this information online. Having various faith traditions expressed from folks who are experts in their respective religious traditions would only strengthen our ability to address trauma. We welcome your input! That being said, we are in the business of helping people regardless of the faith tradition they may or may not hold.

No matter what a person believes, we have found that love, acceptance, encouragement and resolution best come from intimately close horizontal and vertical relationships. Our hope is that we can build a relationship with you, even in reading this book.

We've got your back, you are not alone, and we will not leave you behind!

AUTHOR'S NOTE

Although well trained, I'm not sure I was well prepared for deployment. There comes a point in everyone's deployment when it hits you: this is real. Degrees, accolades, ribbons, devices and honors mean nothing when it comes to what we see and experience. My older brother Joe, a 4th degree black belt in jiu-jitsu and Vietnam veteran, made this very clear to me at an early age. The only belt that matters in a fight is the one that keeps your pants up. I love how Vietnam veterans think.

I entered the military as a psychologist after the attacks of 9/11. I was so furious by what I saw that I wasn't about to stand by and do nothing. After being on the cover of the Air Force *Citizen Airman* magazine for an innovative treatment of PTS(D), I volunteered to deploy to Kandahar, Afghanistan, because I didn't want to be a provider who didn't know what it's like to go to war. I joined to serve and make a difference.

While in a war zone, I saw and experienced firsthand the devastating effects of war. I have the deepest respect for our men and women who fight this battle on a continual basis, who experience the full impact of trauma on the psyche and the family. We, the American people, owe them a debt beyond anything we can ever repay. They are willing to sacrifice their lives for this country, and they deserve anything and everything a true servant and warrior should have. I hope you feel the same.

CONTENTS

CHAPTER 1: SOMETIMES, WE ARE BROKEN

Broken, and trained not to ask for help. That is the real issue many of our warriors deal with today. Growing up, how often did we hear, "Bend, but don't break?" But one has to ask, why did someone have to come up with that slogan in the first place? Most likely because people were clearly at their breaking point. No doubt the decrease in military-end strength has increased the number of deployments for military personnel. And if you don't believe there is a draft, tell that to the people who experienced stop-loss when they tried to get out. This all-volunteer military were not allowed to do so. This shift went from volunteer to "voluntold." Let that sink in for a moment.

Today's combat veterans know all too well the motto that keeps us from asking for help. We hear it over and over, "Pain is weakness leaving the body." We hear other such statements: "Don't let the guy next to you down," "Bring everyone home alive," "Leave no one behind." We take these to heart; we believe them; we live them; we will risk life and limb to abide by them – and we will die for them.

There are times when we are put into situations where there is no good outcome – no way to win. We are also required to follow orders with which we may inherently disagree. On the battlefield, we are forced into immediate, ethical dilemmas with life and death as the final outcome. And most often, there is very little time to contemplate a win-win scenario, even if that were possible. Most decisions are based on circumstances, circumstances we cannot control or even influence. And action must be taken. As an example, in the context of war, if someone drives through a checkpoint, what do we do? How do we respond? Why didn't they stop? Didn't they see the sign? Is this a valid threat? What do I do? Whatever I choose, I lose. They lose. JUST STOP!

Rules of engagement:

- M-16 warning shot
- They didn't stop.
- Won't stop.
- Engage.
- Shoot into engine block.
- Adrenaline
- Now closer
- Mitigate risk.
- Repeat fire.
- Smoke
- Chaos
- Death
- Investigation
- It was a dad, a mom and two kids.
- Why?

These are the life and death decisions that haunt us. And then, the "what if" questions arise – the relentless questions for which we have no answers.

There are other descriptions besides "broken" that we relate to: shattered, confused, depleted, pained, exhausted, changed forever, hopeless, lost, on autopilot, no longer the person we once were.

Going to war changes a person at the core. And there is no going back. Retreat is not an option.

One way or another, there is only forward.

WILL WE EVER BE THE SAME?

Deployment changes people. PERIOD. What I have seen so often is that family members, friends, and deployed personnel all know that those who have been deployed are not the same persons they once were. Their lives, their perspectives, their moral compass, even their souls are affected. It is as if they are a Navy destroyer on a mission, but they are off course and run aground, stuck, isolated, feeling vulnerable, unable to utilize all of their resources and firepower.

It is no wonder that people reach a point where they feel as if they are broken with no answer in sight. Demons of darkness can be unrelenting. Sometimes people reach a point where they just want it all to go away. They no longer want to feel the pain and sting of haunting memories and their gut-wrenching guilt. They no longer want to be a burden to those they love. They just want to be left alone, cause no more harm, and go peacefully into the night.[1] They want to dispatch the demons that inhabit the darkness that now occupies their soul.

---

[1] In a poem, author Dylan Thomas (1952, *In Country Sleep and other poems*, New Directions) encourages old men to defy death and rage against the end of life. It was personal because his own father was dying at the time. Less than two years later, the author drank himself to death at the age of 39. In contrast, young warriors see death as an opportunity to avoid a continuation of the pain created by their participation in war.

When we join the military, we have ideals – very high ideals – about right and wrong, and the conviction that it is our job to mitigate evil. But somehow, in the fog of war,[2] our moral compass can sometimes veer off without our even realizing it, and we can become like those we are fighting against; the ones who witness and then sometimes participate in indescribable atrocities. We experience and see things that painfully remind us of our own actions, our own decisions, our own failures. There is no sanctuary, no serenity, no peace. We long for peace and rest, but it does not come. Our memories haunt us, and we feel an intense need to punish ourselves for allowing our humanity to be deceived and manipulated by the reality of combat which seldom allows the voice of compassion and grace to be heard.

And so, we turn inward, toward our very soul, knowing that we have betrayed more than just humanity; we have betrayed ourselves, and we have betrayed God. As if we even believe in such a deity anymore. It is in this state that we want to slip quietly into non-existence. Or we wish to personally feel the heat of a bullet in our heart or head so that we can feel what others have had to feel. In this way, we are convinced, we will feel better; that relief will come because we have gotten what we deserve – the cold, sharp, burning edge of death by cop, or from our own hands, or from slamming our truck into a bridge.

Our thoughts bring about feelings we have desperately tried to avoid. We do not want to feel because the only feeling we experience is pain – intense, dark pain. It is as if we are forced to carefully and delicately walk barefoot on broken glass, all the while hearing the shards crackling beneath us. Our blood oozes, and we feel the pain with every step we take. But we cannot stand still, and

---

[2] Clausewitz, "Fog of War"

so we press on in the hopes to find grass or anything where we can pull the glass from our feet and make the pain stop.

We think about the explosions and screams of those who died stepping onto IEDs. We feel the reverberation and shock waves of an RPG which vibrates our inner being and blows out our eardrums until the ringing is so loud it is deafening. Our friends and family try to intervene, but we cannot hear you. And no matter how hard we try to ask for help, it is as if we are trapped inside our body[3] asking, begging for help, but unable to move or let any sound escape our lips. No one can hear our screams. And no one comes to our rescue.

Instead, we are told, "Thank you for your service."

Why? Because loved ones, friends, and even strangers have no idea what else to say. And what *service* is that? The service that is cause for our regret? The opposite of righteousness and honor. We stare straight ahead and want to say, "You have no idea where I've been, what I've seen, and what I've done. Not only have I seen evil up close and personal, but I also wonder if it is I who I see in the mirror. Have I committed the unforgiveable sin? Is all lost? Is there any hope remaining? If grace is real, is there any left for me?"

The atrocities we visualize do not stop. They are permanently embedded in our mind. So, we escape through any means possible. We avoid at all costs anything that reminds us of this raw, pinpricking of our soul. We desperately need and want help, but it is as if we have to rip the duct tape from a gaping painful wound to even get to the problem. And when we do finally ask for help, we have no confidence that the right medical or mental health intervention will fix the problem. Where is our answer? Where is

---

[3]Sleep paralysis is such an example. I've personally experienced falling asleep and not being able to physically move, all while being haunted by nightmares that I desperately wanted to escape. It's similar to being given curare for surgery and only afterward does the doctor learn that you felt every cut but couldn't move to alert him to stop.

our hope? Where will the healing salve that we desperately need come from? We are not only hurting; we are shattered and broken.

THERE IS NO TIME TO WASTE

By the time you have finished reading the first two chapters in this book, one more veteran will have killed himself or herself. By the time you finish this book, at least five more veterans will have made the ultimate decision to stop trying, to just end the struggle, to quit.

It is this mission for which we must provide an answer. And although painful and not without personal risk, we venture to speak with authority, even though there are times when it is best not to make a single sound. There is no doubt the critics will rise in protest. But enough is enough, something must be done to curb our pain and the suicides. And instead of arguing in protest like the Vietnam war, consider your own solution to moral injury and trauma. Maybe God will use you to help those in need. Maybe instead of asking, "Why doesn't God do something?" God is asking, "Why don't you do something?"

We need to hear from the voices of those who have been there, who will stand next to us and remind us that we are not alone, we are not forgotten, that there are real answers, and all will be okay in this world.

I want you to know that there truly is a hope and a future.

It is to that end that I pen the words in this book. I firmly and unconditionally believe that there truly is hope, grace, love, unconditional acceptance and forgiveness, even for us.

You may have heard, "As a man thinketh, so is he."[4] Well, the thoughts that influence our lives can come from at least three very different origins:

1. Internally
2. Externally
3. Delusional/psychotic, sometimes evil thinking

INTERNAL THOUGHTS

First are the internal thoughts that we say to ourselves. These are the thoughts we hear inside our head. These we not only hear internally, but we have also often accepted and believed them. You know them, you've thought them, you've heard them loud and clear. It is our mind trying to make sense of the world, especially given what we have seen. They are the thoughts and statements that make us who we are. They can be either positive or negative. It can be a small, quiet voice, often times even in a war zone when chaos is all around that says, "Be still and know that I am God." Or it can be a loud voice that demands immediate action, "ENGAGE!" Whether positive or negative, it is these voices that drive our behavior.

These voices are the ones that we once trusted implicitly, that provided us with our moral compass and our way home. But now, maybe now, they are voices that we do not trust, especially given the decisions we have made and the outcomes that have occurred. We question our ability to make decisions. We question the internal voices and what they say we should do. We have been trained in the military to take life when our childhood voices have told us the exact opposite. It is the struggle from "Thou shalt not kill,"[5] to

---

[4] Proverbs 23:7

7

"hesitate and you die!" This is often where conflicts of beliefs evolve and live. This is the crux of where our work lies ahead.

EXTERNAL THOUGHTS

Second, unrelenting thoughts can come from external, outside influences. These are the statements that others have told us, often repeatedly, that we cannot get out of our head. No matter how hard we try, we cannot escape their grasp. They, too, can be positive or negative.   Some of you have heard them from parents or grandparents. Some voices have been encouraging: "You've got this," "You can do it," "I love you," "I will never leave you." These external voices can be internalized to the point that we not only hear them, but we also accept and believe them.

Unfortunately, there are also negative voices that we hear from people as well. Things like, "You will never amount to anything," "You are a loser," "You were a mistake," "I don't even know why you were born." In our adult, military life, it may turn to "You are a grunt and nothing else," "You failed the mission," "You failed your men," "You are a failure and disgrace to the uniform." When we accept these voices as truth, it can create a horribly negative view of self, depression and feelings of worthlessness and hopelessness.

DELUSIONAL/PSYCHOTIC SOMETMES EVIL THINKING

---

5 In reality, the original language says, "Thou shalt not murder." Killing and murder are two very different things. This is a short synopsis as a complete discussion would go beyond the scope and intent of this book. For example, to kill innocent women and children such as what happened in "My Lai" is inexcusable. This experience is actually where the term "unlawful order" was founded. Opposite this is to kill someone whose intent is to destroy you, especially when one is legally and morally justified.

Finally, there are times when we have thoughts that we can't even fathom having, thoughts that seem to come out of nowhere and that are so foreign, we dare not even speak of them. Oftentimes, they are of killing others. We plot, we plan, we strategize. And then we wonder what in the world are we thinking. God calls them "fiery darts." They are not from within; they are literally thoughts from outside us.

And how are we to handle such voices? God calls us to extinguish them and to do so quickly, to literally plunge the fiery dart into water and let it smolder out. We speculate that we are to extinguish them quickly, for as you linger with these voices, the more devastating the impact. Analogous to an infection, the faster we ingest an antibiotic, the sooner the infection is destroyed.

Some of us have experienced negative voices because we have seen evil up close and personal. We have to deal with atrocities we could previously have only imagined. The strongest voices are those attached to memories, things we have seen and things we have done. But not only is it the memories and the voices, it is also the anchored emotions that will not give way. The reliving of memories are permanent pictures cauterized in our brains. It is the thoughts and emotions attached to these memories of what we have seen, experienced and now want to avoid at all cost. They are the nightmares that come like a thief in the night to steal away our peace and rest.

They can be daunting to the point of sheer terror. They are voices we thought we would never hear. "Do it, just do it" when we sit there with a gun sitting next to us. "Go on, pick it up," says the voice. 1 bullet, 6 chambers, "spin it," and Russian roulette is on. The voices can be unrelenting. And for some, it is literally a nightmare in high definition. We hear them and try to block them out, and yet they are unrelenting for a reason. They speak to us in a very clear voice: "It's time," "Just do it," "Get it over with," "You can't do it, can you?" "You are a failure," "You can't even kill yourself," "You will never be anything but a failure."

Is it possible that these fiery darts can be similar to negative thoughts we've been told and sometimes believe? Most definitely. Could it be from what others deem as evil trying to thwart humanity? Certainly. Could it even be from hopelessness where we feel that there is no answer, no solution to our never-ending guilt? Yes. But whatever their etiology, wherever they come from, they must be extinguished.

Have you heard them? Have you struggled to extinguish them? Remember: you are not alone, and we will not leave you behind.

TIME FOR A DIFFERENT APPROACH

It is time to explore a different approach to hope and healing – one that takes into account the full array of thoughts and emotions that churn inside us in our relentless pursuit of serenity. We hear the words "compassion," "forgiveness," and "grace," but do not feel they are for us. Or, maybe it is the voices inside us whose strategy is to keep us from finding peaceful rest. No matter where the thoughts or fiery darts come from, this is our *New Mission*.

We are called, instead, to listen to the voices that bring about grace, love, and forgiveness all while honoring those who have made the ultimate sacrifice. We do not have to blame ourselves, beat ourselves up in some sadistic manner in order to somehow feel as if justice is being served. They are not mutually exclusive. We can accomplish both. There is a better way. A much better way. But let's be clear: negative voices will not go peacefully into the night. We must subdue them and conquer them as we do the enemy. Fiery darts do not extinguish easily or quietly. It is a battle that wages a war of not only the mind, but also the soul.

CHAPTER 2: THE THOUSAND-YARD STARE

Intent: To help combat veterans understand the reason they may become isolated, feel disconnected, and do whatever they can to avoid the intense and raw emotions experienced from war. At Project Healing Heroes, our intent is to create veteran-focused, specific therapeutic interventions that go beyond current therapies to address the most difficult raw emotions that military members experience. These include survivor guilt, moral injury, and grief and loss, to name just a few.

Allow me to share with you the story of Michael. I saw this 19-year-old Army private in the USO in Kandahar, Afghanistan, when he was sitting on a couch, exhausted, wearing a dirty uniform, and appearing to look as if he were watching television. In reality, he had that thousand-yard stare that people talk about. I'd only heard of it. I had not seen it face to face. I came to Afghanistan as a mental health provider not only to serve, but also to learn firsthand what it's like to go to war. So, I sat down next to him. I wanted to learn, and I wanted to help. I decided to engage him in a conversation.

I asked, "Where are you from?" He didn't respond. I asked again, wondering if he hadn't heard me. Still no response. "Well, this is awkward," I thought. After a few seconds which seemed like an eternity, I decided to try one more time, although I was starting to question myself. "Howdy soldier, where are you from?" hoping my southern language might increase his confidence in trusting me. Very slowly, he turned his head in my direction and tried to focus his gaze, all while blinking rapidly. He quietly stared at my rank, then looked me in the eye while still blinking and responded, "Kentucky," and with a deep sigh repeated, "I'm from... Kentucky."

This conversation wasn't going as I had hoped. In my decision to deploy, part of why I did so was to understand what people go through in war and to do whatever I could to help. So, here I was, in the USO, trying to talk to someone I had never met, and it wasn't going very well. I wasn't sure if I should continue, but I thought, "why not?" I had come halfway around the world to try to make a difference. I needed to meet people where they were and learn how to best serve them.

I decided to ask a follow-up question. "Kentucky, huh? Great basketball team," I said. He nodded. Yeah, this was going great. So, I tried one last time as I didn't want to be any more intrusive into his life than I already was. "How long have you been here?" He sighed, twice actually, the latter sigh being drawn out more than the first. "Well, Major, I've been here for four months, but we are heading home next week," he replied.

This response caught me off guard. I had heard of trauma surgeons and other medical professionals deploying for only four months, but not the regular Army. In my limited experience, they usually do 12 or even 18 months. Surprised, I replied, "Wow, I didn't know the Army was only deploying people for four months at a time."

Although tired and weary and more patient with me than he should have been, he shifted his eyes, which had returned to my rank, looked straight at me and said, "Well, we don't normally, but half of my platoon has been killed. We are supposed to redeploy next week, but I don't even know if I will be alive next week."

Now my attention was even more focused than before.

He continued, "But that's not what gets me."

Curious, I asked, "What does?"

"I'm now on point, which means every time I take a step, I ask myself, 'Will this be my last step, will this be my last step, will this be my last step?' I just pray I make it home alive. I didn't come here to die. I came here to serve."

I just sat there. I'm a trained clinical psychologist, but at that moment I had no answers. I simply didn't know what to say. What could I possibly say? Who am I to even speak? Half his platoon has been killed, and he feared death that very well could be around the corner or buried under the ground in the form of an IED. He didn't want to be there, and I tried to understand, at least the best I could, but I'd never walked in this 19-year-old kid's shoes (or boots). He had seen more death than any 19-year-old should ever see.

Maybe you are a lot smarter than I. Probably so, to be honest. Maybe you have some ideas about what you would have said at that moment. If so, I would have loved to have been wearing one of those earpieces that newscasters have during live broadcasts so that you could whisper some words of wisdom that would have helped me. But at that moment, I had nothing. There I was, a man trained at the highest levels in human behavior about what to say, and I just sat there, feeling that if I said the wrong thing, I would possibly make matters even worse. And that was the last thing I wanted to do. I'd come to Afghanistan to do the opposite. My compassion for what he was going through overwhelmed me, and I couldn't say a word.

We just breathed.

Chaplains speak of a ministry of presence, about just being there with a person. I'd experienced something very similar when a friend of our family sat at our table the night my mother passed away. He said, "I'm here for you. Anything you need, anything at all" and sat there the whole day. Just that statement and his presence were extremely comforting. But with that soldier, I felt as if I were completely useless. As I sat there, and we breathed together, I was trying to make sense of my own cognitive dissonance – where two opposing beliefs compete. I wanted to be helpful, but I had nothing helpful to say. This issue of cognitive dissonance will be more thoroughly defined and discussed throughout this book.

Part of my intent is to help find a solution to our competing thought processes, one in which resolution is found and not simply left hanging. This book is about the mission of doing just that: finding resolution.

THE IMPACT OF WAR

The story of Michael is unfortunate but not unusual. When military personnel go on missions, they are, more often than we like to admit, put in harm's way. The psychological effects can be devastating. When this happens repeatedly, our mind has to decide how to react and respond. The very real threat that you or a buddy may be killed is often the norm on deployment. Unfortunately, in theater, we have a mission to do and very little time to process our thoughts. Plus, we are trained not to think. "To think is to die" is what we are told. Their motive is good in that delaying, even for a split second, could cost a life, but psychologically, it's devastating.

The problem with training is that no matter how much you receive, you know it's not real. It's very hard to simulate real war. The closer you get to it, the higher the risk of someone dying, even in training. Just this week, another soldier died in a plane crash during a training operation. The challenge is that you truly never know what a person is going to do under intense stress and pressure. For example, we can train and retrain our military to respond to a particular situation, but until they are actually in it, we don't know how a person is going to react. It's very difficult to simulate the reactions that snipers, medics, infantry personnel, doctors, nurses, gunners, or other health care professionals who deal with life and death on a daily basis will have. What we are told is, "What you are experiencing is a normal reaction to an abnormal situation." And that situation is war. Unfortunately, people often begin to believe that this is a *normal* stress situation. Let me make something perfectly clear: *war is not normal.*

While at the Role 3, Trauma Level 1 center in Kandahar, the commander made it very clear that he wanted even his best trauma surgeons, nurses, techs, etc., to leave the Area of Responsibility (AOR) after four months. When I queried him about this, he told me, "Because after a while people begin to think this is normal, that this is life. It is not; it is WAR." Veterans of a combat zone will repeatedly say, "You don't understand; you've never been there." And for most people, that is true. Most Americans have not experienced the devastating effects of war. And even if they have, every person and every situation is different.

Part of the challenge is that when you have been through war and seen people injured and killed, especially a battle buddy and/or a good friend, you begin to distance yourself from your emotions. It's a form of self-preservation. We do this to survive. That is normal. In psychology, the term is desensitization. And desensitization can lead to dissociation. So can intense trauma. What is specific to combat trauma is that it doesn't have to be just one traumatic experience. It can be a deployment of experiences, which is key to how treatment should be done.

Simply put, it is not normal to think that death and injury are a normal way of life. They are not! They are a part of life and a part of war, but they are not *life*. Tell military members, though, that what they experienced in war isn't real, and they will say it is more real than anything they have ever experienced in their life. We have to differentiate between feeling alive and accepting that war is normal. You might need to ponder that last statement for a moment.

What we should say is that we don't want to get to a point where we think that death, destruction, and injury are normal. We didn't fight this war against terrorism so that we can start believing that this is all there is, that *this* is the new normal. **It is a normal part of life, yes, but it is not normal life.**

In my previous book, *The Combat PTS(D) Resilience and Reintegration Workbook*, we discussed two rules of war:

Rule #1: People die in war.
Rule #2: You cannot change rule #1.

Of course, there are more rules, but if you cannot accept these basic rules, you will constantly be fighting a war within. What we struggle most with is acceptance that this is beyond our ability to control. We will discuss that in later chapters.

DEPERSONALIZATION

Part of the challenge of trying to figure out our emotions when we witness death is determining what is normal and what is not. For example, I will often ask military members to raise their hands in response to the following questions:

1. How many of you experience sleeping problems?
2. How many of you experience irritability?
3. Anger outbursts?

4. Rage?
5. How many of you get angry watching television, the news – or quit watching all together?
6. How many of you feel you are not the same person as before, that you've changed?
7. How many of you experience nightmares?
8. How many of you experience flashbacks?
9. How many of you feel as if you left unfinished business?
10. That you would want to go back?
11. How many of you use avoidance?
12. Numbing?
13. Isolation?
14. How many of you believe people would be shocked or judge you if you told them what is actually going on in your head?
15. How many of you don't talk about things because it's safer to keep it to yourself?

When I ask these questions, combat veterans raise their hands to at least 12 of the 15 questions, and most raise their hand to all of them. Then I ask, "Are you normal?"
The best response I've had to date is, "Yes, if you are a combat veteran."

Although every person in theater has a very different experience, I wanted to begin this book by describing a situation that I had no idea how to address psychologically, at least initially. I like the tough questions, the ones that people have that are at the core of their being, because if I can find an answer to those, I feel confident I can help answer the others.

CHAPTER 3: CAN A DRONE PILOT HAVE PTS(D)?

D o you believe that a drone pilot can get PTSD? Yes or No? (Circle your answer.) Why/why not? Please either write an answer or ponder it. _____

_____

When a person is wrong, the best thing that person can do is admit it. I was wrong! Very wrong. I work with combat veterans who have PTS(D), and yet I did not believe that a person who was a drone pilot could experience PTS(D). My logic made sense to me. Drone pilots are safe, usually at an Air Force base, thousands of miles away from their targets. They get to go to lunch at the restaurant across the street, come back to work, and resume their mission. I knew they put in significant amounts of time at their job, but honestly, wasn't it like watching a real-life video game? You fly an airplane you are not in, you have an aerial view from 5,000 miles away, you are safe in the U.S., you do this day in and day out, and there is a lot of downtime during which nothing happens. You are very much like a police officer who does his job, knowing that he *could* die, but mostly experience intense boredom sprinkled with spurts of incredible chaos. But in the case of the drone pilot, you are in one of the safest and most secure facilities in the world with not a single threat to your life. So how in the world does a drone pilot experience PTS(D)?

DESENSITIZATION

One combat veteran I met through the Disabled American Veterans (DAV), and who gave me permission to use his story, completely changed my mind, my life, and the way I do therapy. It was a typical day at work for him—flying missions over Afghanistan, talking with his buddies, and following up on intelligence leads that might or might not pan out. Drone pilots are notorious for celebrating a "kill." They not only feel the intense pressure and rush, but also others around them actually celebrate with them when an enemy combatant is "eliminated." There are high fives all around with cheering in celebration. A lot of distance is involved (actually halfway around the world), and we have just celebrated another person's death. Enemy combatant or not, that "kill" being celebrated is a person who was killed by the pilot's own hands (or fingers).

We resolve this matter in our heads by telling ourselves they are the enemy. They are trying to kill us, and it's better them than us. The more we kill, the less chance there is that our guys will die. This is desensitization[6] to human life (or death) at its worst. In

---

[6] Desensitization occurs when you become less sensitive to stimulus. It can be positive or negative. Through repeated exposure to human suffering, some can become less sensitive to that suffering, able to watch a starving child without being moved to offer care for that child. In a war environment, it may be necessary and even helpful to become desensitized to human suffering in order to complete the mission, but after returning home, that soldier may no longer respond with the same degree of compassion to his children, or other loved ones, and destroys the relationship over time.

reality, many drone pilots feel as if they shouldn't be celebrating having just killed another human being, especially when they first experience this situation. Where else would we celebrate another person's death and actually be encouraged to do so by those around us? Only a sociopath would think this way, right? No. It's our human mind trying to make sense of war. We become, out of necessity, desensitized. It is our way of protecting our mind.

Have you noticed any desensitization in your own life with what you experienced in war? If so, how? _____

_____

Have you intentionally tried to stay away from things that trigger emotions or thinking about things so as not to have to deal with them? Or possibly used illicit or legally prescribed drugs to not have to feel? Do you feel as if you have become numb?

Part of the challenge we face is that by suppressing these feelings, it is the total opposite of resilience. Unfortunately, when we don't address these issues, they come out in other ways. The symptoms are similar to the warning lights on the dashboard of a car. When the lights come on, it's not a good idea to ignore them, pull the fuse, or bust them out. Doing so will only lead to more, and possibly worse, long-term problems. And it certainly won't bring about resolution. The reality is that refusing to acknowledge these issues is exactly what keeps us from finding resolution.

Note: Some of the exercises in this text may stir some raw emotions within you. If you feel uncomfortable while doing them, you may wish to stop and move ahead in the text without completing them. You may not be ready to do that exercise at this point. It is okay. Later on, when you feel ready, return and complete it. If you start to feel the raw emotions, it may be better to stop the exercise and try to label precisely what you are feeling and process why you are feeling it, especially if you have a family member, friend or therapist you trust. It may be helpful to you to understand what it is that is causing the distress.

Honestly think about what memories, emotions, thoughts, or feelings you have buried deep down inside. For those who like to write things out, feel free to engage; otherwise, just think about it.

Did you give it some thought? What went through your mind?

The truth is, it hurts. It hurts to think about these things, but we cannot eliminate the infection if we ignore the problem. And yes, it is like ripping duct tape off a wound. We know it's going to hurt. Most physicians will tell you that to eradicate an infection, you not only have to provide antibiotics to eliminate the infection, but you may also have to cut away at the skin until it bleeds. Then fresh blood can come to the rescue and heal the affected area. But if you are anything like most people, you just want to say, "Stay away. Don't touch. It hurts." But all the while, the people who know what it will take have to dig and cut around the infected area to bring about true healing. It is far better to strategically have someone who is an expert help you clean out the infection than to simply rip off the duct tape and hope for the best, or, even worse, have your confidence and trust in someone who fails you at your time of need. If you thought counseling was easy, it's not. Therapy is hard work. Dealing with things you would rather avoid or forget about is emotionally draining. But remember, your new mission is to get better. And I will get you there, as long as you are willing to put in the work.

If one particular issue keeps you up at night, something that occurs repeatedly, it is probably unresolved. You have to do the one act you don't want to do. Think about it, and then write it down. We need to know specifically what it is so that we know what needs healing. In order to know what kinds of wounds we are dealing with, we need to know how deep those wounds go. So, please take the time it takes – even if you need to put this book down and come back to it later —write it down. This book will be here waiting for you when you are ready.

WRITE A SHORT SYNOPSIS OF THE SITUATION.

_____

_____

_____

_____

_____

_____

_____

What emotions or feelings came to the surface when you wrote about this situation that keeps you awake at night? Sadness, depression, hurt, anger, frustration, irritability, worthlessness, shame, guilt, all of the above? What is the precise emotion? Anger might be a good start, but anger can be broken down even further. Are you in a rage, just upset, or somewhere in between? Labeling your emotions may not be comfortable for you, but it can be a useful exercise that helps you learn to deal better with the flooding of emotions that can overwhelm us. The more precise our language we use to describe our feelings, the more precise the scalpel we can use in the healing.

THINK ABOUT AND WRITE ABOUT YOUR SPECIFIC EMOTIONS THAT SURFACE.

_____

_____

_____

CHAPTER 4: IMMINENT DANGER – CONVERGENCE OF MORAL INJURY AND SURVIVOR GUILT

When drone pilots fly hours upon hours with nothing happening, they can become bored. And what happens when a person becomes bored? They become complacent. It's one of the most challenging issues to confront. You sit there in your pilot chair, and nothing happens—miles of flying and hours of terrain and boredom. You have situational awareness on thousands of miles, just flying. You can actually communicate with combat veterans, who are often on convoys, on the ground. They get to know you and you them, all via voice, so you fly and fly and fly as their Overwatch. You are present at any point to intervene and help take out threats so that they have some form of protection, even if it is a half a world away. Then one day it happens.

ALL HELL BREAKS LOOSE

You are listening to your coms, and you hear mass chaos. Insurgents have decided to deploy Rule #1: people are going to die. But you are Overwatch, and it is your job to stop Rule #1, at least on our side, and turn that rule back onto the enemy. The people you watch over are your responsibility, your job, your mission, but the insurgents try to thwart that at all costs, and they have a voice. I wrote "Module XI: THE ENEMY HAS A VOICE" in my book, *The Combat PTS(D) Resilience and Reintegration Workbook*, just to address this issue.

At *their* opportune time, *the enemy* makes the decision to engage. Whatever happens, the reality is people are going to die. You just want it to be bad guys, not our guys.

You do whatever you can to make that happen. You deploy sidewinder missiles at the push of a button to the tune of $420,000 each,[7] all to ensure we kill them before they kill us. This is our plan. This is how we wage war. The "O" (operational) plans are to be executed accordingly. Unfortunately, not all O plans come together the way we design them.

On this particular mission, you, the drone operator, and the convoy are talking when the insurgent attacks begin. Massive chaos ensues, and the fight is on. Through your headset, you hear the bursts of fire, the explosions, the fighting. On and on it goes, but you have to sit there and do whatever you can with whatever information you have, waiting to engage the enemy. But if you deploy your weapon too close, you risk friendly fire. Given the fighting position, you have no choice but to sit and listen to the chaos and await your coordinates for the execution of orders. It becomes apparent by the communications that our side is taking heavy casualties, and then you hear something you never thought you would hear.

Communication comes across telling you that people are being pulled from their severely damaged vehicles and beheaded. Our men continue the fight, but the insurgents have chosen this place this

---

[7] http://www.fi-aeroweb.com/Defense/Sidewinder.html

time for a reason. They were well prepared. They had the advantage of surprise and timing and weapons with the intent to kill.

Convoys are especially vulnerable for many reasons. On this day, the insurgents are winning. We continue to take heavy casualties, and you don't want to listen, but it is your job to be ready when called upon. This is why you were trained. And this has just become personal. We do not have to be trained to have people's backs in the military. It is innate. It is who we are. Some run away from danger, we run to it! We will fight to the death if that is what it requires. Or in this case, do whatever is necessary to ensure our guys are taken care of.

You are ready and prepared to deploy your weapons, but you also feel totally useless and powerless as you await your orders. The fighting continues with more explosions, more screams for help over the radios. The battle rages for what seems like hours, and more insurgents take advantage of the stopped convoy. They have the advantage, they have the heavy weapons, they have surprise, they are winning, and you sit there, angry, frustrated, ready to deploy help, but you cannot. You have no specific coordinates, and the last action you want to take is to kill your own troops. You have at your ready the buttons to drop an arsenal of weapons - to stop the chaos, to stop – or at least minimize – the enemy's capabilities. But the command has not been given. You know that we are getting hit hard, but there you sit. Powerless.

Then you hear that more and more of our guys are getting pulled from their vehicles and killed. Not only are we taking heavy casualties, but the insurgents are taking prisoners. And you know what that means: our troops will either be tortured or killed. It is happening *right now*. You think about the men and women on the ground, as you listen for coordinates or a command. You live in the U.S. and are safe, but they are half a world away being killed. You can do nothing about it. You think about your mission, the soldiers, the sacrifice, the families, and yet you can do nothing. You slam your first on the edge of your desk, making sure to avoid any contact with your weapon systems.

You didn't join this war to be powerless. You didn't join this war to sit back and do nothing. You joined to make a difference, and yet you can't do anything but sit and listen and hope and pray and wait to unleash the arsenal of weapons you have at your command. You have the ability to stop the enemy, but you have no ability to make the decision to do so. It has to be given. So, you sit with no actionable information and no coordinates. The clock is ticking.

Then you hear them. Those two dreaded words—the words of complete hopelessness, complete exhaustion, and complete acceptance of the fate of those on the ground—the words you never hoped to hear in your career. Two words that mean the difference between life and death. Two words that mean the difference between suffering and mercy. Your breathing gets shallow. It's loud in your headphones but quiet in your spirit. Sadness comes upon you, and time stands still. But you have no choice. You must act. Not to act means mission failure; to act means death.

This is not what you signed up for, but it is your job, your mission, and your command. Not to act means that our guys are going to be overrun, killed, tortured, and/or become prisoners of war. They need you to act, but when you do, they will die. You didn't really even expect it, but you knew things were not going as planned. The reality is that the insurgents are winning. You hear it in the intensity of the voices over the radio, and finally in calm acceptance and a strong voice, the command is given by the commander on the ground — "IMMINENT DANGER."[8]

You stop breathing, and your heart is pounding, but you need to be 100 percent sure. Was that the command? Is that the

---

[8] These are not the actual words used. To use them would put our men and women in the military at risk.

communication? No question. "IMMINENT DANGER" is called again. The weapons you have at your disposal are meant for the enemy, NOT OUR GUYS! But the reason for such a command is situations like this—situations in which there is no way out but death. It is not called lightly; as a matter of fact, it is the command of last resort. It is very much along the lines of taking a cyanide pill. Completely irrevocable. It means there are only two options remaining—either fall into the hands of the enemy and continue to be abused, slaughtered, tortured, and killed, or immediate relief.

We don't usually associate death with instant relief, but that is what it is. It is mercy under fire, instantly removed from pain and suffering because the future is far worse than the present. It means accepting death as a reality.

And so, it is done.

You push the button, and the weapon is deployed. You watch as the missile heads toward the light grey ground and the darker areas where there are silhouettes of people running. It is mere seconds for the missile en route to hit its coordinates. A huge explosion. An incredible flash that lights up your screen. And then small traces of light still burning. People lying on the ground everywhere. No movement. Nothing. Total radio silence. No more transmission, no more pain or suffering. It is finished. You are the Angel of Death.

You sit there, and your heart sinks, and it becomes eerily quiet. The monotony of flying has been dramatically altered. The notion that people think flying a drone is like playing a video game is absurd. It is real life. And real death. And you are the one who fired the weapon.

Thoughts race through your mind. You desperately try not to get emotional. Others around you know you did what you had to do. The room is eerily silent. The audio sounds you normally hear, even those from various parts of the world that are pumped into the room, are slowly and methodically turned down. No one wants to make a sound. You can feel your heart pounding as you breathe in and out. Your chest expands as you take another slow breath. Your eyes gaze straight ahead as you take deep breaths trying not to hyperventilate. You intentionally slow your breath to maintain your bearings until you feel as if you are not even breathing. Sometimes, you even have to remember to breathe. You swallow and your eyes shift from left to right as you scan the room with tears filling your eyes, and then you feel it: a hand on your shoulder, a squeeze of assurance that what you did was the right thing, the strength of a person's hands, squeezing tightly as your shoulders shrink down and you feel completely and utterly defeated. Your chin quivers, and your eyes fill up with tears, trying desperately not to make a whimper.

How can this be happening? This is not what I signed up for. You wet your lips and bite them as if to wonder, "Is this real?" The small pain you feel is something your men will never feel again. They will never feel anything ever again. The touch of their loved one's hands, the hugs they give their kids at night, the embrace of their wife who loves them unconditionally, the warmth of her touch, her soft caress, her head on "their" shoulder. For them, that feeling is gone forever. The void will never be filled. They will never, ever again feel human touch on this earth.

Everyone watches as you get out of your chair. You place your headphones on the control panel. You stare at the black and white screen where you see the white lights and phosphorous of the explosions from the weapons that are meant for the enemy. The men whose bodies are strewn all over the landscape are *your* men, the men you promised to protect. You know it will take time to even recover their bodies. We never leave anyone behind. And yet they are in enemy territory. And then it hits you. Light the whole damn place on fire. Destroy everyone around them. Kill every insurgent who was trying to harm our guys.

You sit down, jam your headphones on, and you unleash every hellfire missile that is left in your arsenal from the drone. You do not have permission to fire, but you do not care. You keep pressing the button until every last one of the missiles has been fired. And you keep hitting that button over and over and over. There are no missiles left, but you do not care. You continue firing repeatedly, knowing there is nothing being released, but your emotions have taken over to the point that you just keep hitting the trigger.

And your friend comes over and puts his hand on yours and slowly lifts it away from the controls. He gently sets your hand on your thigh. You drop your head until your chin feels like it's going to be driven right into your chest. Your shoulders fall and you feel his other hand on your neck and shoulders as he squeezes once again. And then you hear his voice, although it seems as if it is a million miles away, "Come on. Let's get some air."

As you go outside, you look up at the blue sky, you hear the sounds of birds chirping and you wonder what the scene looks like halfway around the world. You are told to go home, take some time off, and people offer to drive you home. Gracefully, you decline the ride. You try to keep your military bearings, but it's hard. This is why we in the military have such structure and training. It is times like these when we rely on our training to carry us through.

You make your way to your car, and you see the familiar territory as you drive home from work in total silence. You finally, somehow, make it home even though you missed your exit. You have completely lost track of space and time.

"So, honey, how was your day?" your wife asks. You look at her, and she knows something is wrong. Terribly wrong. You stand there, immobile, and tears well up. You stiffen your jaw and look straight ahead. You rub your forehead and massage your temples in some sort of self-soothing attempt. Then your shoulders and head drop, and you can no longer keep it in. Tears rolling down your face go to sobbing in an instant. You cannot speak, not just because of your intense emotions, but also because all of what has happened is classified. You are weeping, but there is no true release. You drop to your knees out of sheer emotion. You feel as if you have become the one thing you never ever wanted to become: the Angel of Death.

Questions haunt your every moment. Fiery darts, wherever their etiology, are coming in at you from what seem like all directions. They are honed in right at your mind. They have been in relentless pursuit, and although you have kept them at bay, they seem to now be the victor.

- "How did it come to this? HOW?"
- "How could God let this happen?"
- "Why did they have to be at that place at that time?"
- "Did I hear the call correctly?"
- "Did I make the right decision?"
- "Could I have done anything differently?"
- "I failed my mission."
- "I failed my men."
- "I am the Angel of Death."

The last thing you want is more emotions, more feelings, more of anything. Your apparent attempts at denial from the trauma are now giving way to depersonalization. You don't even feel like yourself – you don't even feel alive. As a matter of fact, you want to go drink and isolate yourself, but even doing that doesn't stop your thoughts from racing. Sleep is elusive, and re-experiencing isn't just a word, it's now your life. Days go by, and you want to feel nothing.

Your friends and family notice that something isn't right, but when they try to get close, you pull away. In your mind, as long as you are not making decisions, people won't die—at least by your hands. You may begin to self-medicate because of the sleepless nights, pain, suffering, and feelings that are simply too much to bear. Who wouldn't?

Your kids may want time with you, to be held, to be comforted, and you look at your hands, and these are the same hands that feel as if they have blood all over them. I wonder if this isn't why Pontius Pilate literally washed his hands after the people had made their wishes known. Barabbas was to be set free, and Jesus was to be crucified. It was these hands that killed OUR troops. It shouldn't be this way. "I shouldn't have done it. I should have disobeyed the order. I should have...," and your mind will not shut off.

Everyone knows something is wrong, but they know you cannot or will not talk about it, so they respect it, but they know you are hurting. It is the war within, invisible, unrelenting, irreversible. People want to touch you, but the last thing you want is comfort, especially when you are the self-proclaimed Angel of Death. You think about those who died that day, that they will never feel the touch of their loved ones again. You feel totally unworthy of love, of acceptance, of anything. You have that thousand-yard stare, just like the guy in Kandahar, and you keep losing track of time, just like when you missed your exit that night. Your command talks with you and tells you that you did the right thing, the admirable thing. You provided mercy, but all you feel is death. There is no relief, no comfort, no forgiveness, nothing.

You are, after all, a trained killer. The last thing you believe is that you can be forgiven. How can you be? How can you be

Overwatch *and* be the one who kills our own troops? This cognitive dissonance where two competing beliefs about who you are and what you are supposed to do will not stop. It feels as if you are standing in cement that is drying, and the longer you linger in these thoughts, the heavier your legs become, and the more trapped you feel. Moral injury has taken its grip around you and refuses to let go. Your life has been forever altered. Or, at least, it feels that way.

> Would you blame a person in this state if they felt like making it all go away? Many people at this point begin to have suicidal thoughts. And, over time, those thoughts turn into plans. They feel as if they would be better off dead or at least out of pain where they can never again cause others pain. They feel that nobody understands them, or they think they will be judged, and convince themselves accordingly. But hang on, there is hope.

My combat drone pilot left that horrible day in a confused, altered, dissociative state with no future, no hope, and tremendous guilt. If it were me, I would be experiencing almost every PTS(D) symptom known to man. This is why I have changed my mind about who can and who cannot experience PTS(D). Can a drone pilot have PTS(D)? WITHOUT QUESTION!

NOW WHAT?

If you were that person, how would you have dealt with the competing beliefs about who you are? Are you not *Overwatch*? Are you not supposed to do everything you can to protect our troops?

Then how can you in good conscience kill Americans, your fellow brothers in arms? How?

It is no wonder in trying to resolve these moral issues that people end up very distraught and confused. They are constantly trying to make sense of what they have done and who they believe they have become. For in the end, it is they who have to look at themselves in the mirror and answer to God for their actions. It is they who stare straight ahead and wonder, "How could I have done such a thing?" It is the dichotomous position of seeing oneself as a person who protects others and yet killed the very people he was protecting.

This is but one small example of how moral injury occurs in combat. One of many, many such examples.

This world is very complex. We sometimes find ourselves doing things we never thought we would do or, for some of us, not taking action when we feel we should have. This action or inaction leaves us questioning and confused. We may wonder how we could possibly have done such a thing. We are literally trying to make sense of something that does not make sense. Although it is impossible to hold two opposing beliefs at the same time, we do not give up easily in doing so. For some of you, the Angel of Death belief is more heavily weighted than the Angel of Mercy. I think those who've experienced similar circumstances and read this might be able to relate.

Moral injury is being raised with a certain belief system and then transgressing against that very system. There are significant consequences to this. Because we are raised by our parents, family, friends, church and others, it sometimes brings us up against the very things that we are anchored to that keep us morally strong and rock solid. And when that anchor seems to have left us, we feel completely and totally adrift, often alone in our head, and worse.

The details and circumstances of your situation may not be the same as the drone pilot's, but those of you who have experienced it know what I'm talking about. The internal conflict of your beliefs – those you grew up with and the ones you've violated. If it were you in the drone pilot's shoes, how would you feel, what would you think, what would be going through your mind?

I'm going to ask some very pointed questions. Please answer them honestly.

1. Do you view the drone pilot as the Angel of Death or the Angel of Mercy? Why?

    _____

    _____

    _____

    _____

2. If you were the drone pilot, would you say anything to people you trusted? Would you worry more about OPSEC than yourself? Once again, it's an example of conflicting beliefs. If you did choose to say something, what would you share?

    _____

    _____

    _____

    _____

3. Do you believe this drone pilot is at risk for suicide? Yes or No (please circle). If yes, what are some of the signs you would be concerned about?

    _____

    _____

    _____

    _____

4. If you were the drone pilot, what statements would you be making about yourself? What thoughts do you think would be going through your mind? Whom would you blame?

_____

_____

_____

_____

5. What if you were one of the convoy's family members, and you found out what happened. What would you say to the drone pilot if given the opportunity? And as the drone pilot, given the same opportunity, what would you say to the convoy's family members?

_____

_____

_____

_____

6. What could you possibly say to the family member that would make a difference?

_____

_____

_____

_____

7. Do you believe the deceased's family members might blame the drone pilot?

_____

_____

8. If this had happened to you, could you forgive yourself? Why? Why not?

_____

_____

_____

_____

9. What symptoms do you think this drone pilot had? How would you mitigate against them?

_____

_____

_____

_____

10. What do your spiritual beliefs say about you at this moment? Does God judge you? Do you judge yourself?

_____

_____

_____

_____

Your situation may be similar or very different. Maybe you were the one on the ground. Maybe it was you on a convoy. Maybe you were the boots on the ground kicking in doors. If so, let's take some time to write down what happened to you. You need to tell your story.

I have found that sometimes people need to write everything that happened verbatim, and other times they need a little guidance. If you want to just write what happened, by all means, write. Below is some space to make that happen. If, on the other hand, you would like some direction and guidance, or more structure, consider using the REACH worksheet (below). Either way, you need to write down what you've experienced.

My Trauma Account:

_____

_____

_____

_____

_____

_____

_____

_____

_____

_____

_____

_____

_____

_____

_____

_____

_____

_____

_____

Resiliency for Emotional and Cognitive Health – Veterans Education Training System (REACH VETS) Worksheet

Aspects of Situation	Belief	Context	Differing Opinions	Emotional cost
Who or what brought me to this point?	I believe _____	Who was involved? _____	Reasons why I convinced myself that my belief is true. (Prosecuting attorney arguments: what would JAG say?):	What percentage of time does this issue take away from my life? _____ %
			1. _____	# of jobs lost _____
		When did it happen?	2. _____	# of relationships lost _____
		2. _____	3. _____	Rate Emotions based on your Belief and what %
	Because _____	3. _____	4. _____	
		4. _____	5. _____	___ / ___
		Where did it happen?	Reasons why my belief is not 100% true. (Defense attorney argument/ self-defense):	___ / ___
		5. _____	1. _____	___ / ___
	Therefore (consequence, how does this belief affect me or others) _____	Why did it happen?	2. _____	Factors (please circle):
		_____	3. _____	All- or- nothing thinking: Y/N
			4. _____	Mind reading: Y/N
			5. _____	Emotional logic: Y/N
			6. _____	Overgeneralizing: Y/N
				Defense mechanism: Y/N
				General themes (examples):
				☐ Anger ☐ Grief & Loss
				☐ Avoidance ☐ Guilt
				☐ Depression ☐ Safety
				☐ Failure ☐ Shame
				☐ Fear ☐ Power/Control
				☐ Forgiveness ☐ Trust
				☐ _____

Healthy Resilient Thought: I now **choose** to believe _____. Therefore, _____, because _____.

Now, go back to Emotional cost, and rerate your %, assuming that if you could tell yourself this mantra, over time, with genuineness, it could be true.

38

CHAPTER 5: LEFT FOR DEAD - A BLACKHAWK PILOT'S NIGHTMARE COMES TRUE

A friend of mine named Jay was kind enough to share a story that I believe gets to the heart of survivor guilt and moral injury, as well as grief and loss. Our intent is not to shower you with stories but to help you grasp the enormity of the mental challenges our combat veterans face. It is also designed to help us all better understand the complexity of trauma and why combat veterans may struggle with cognitive dissonance and competing belief systems. Some of the information has been changed to protect privacy.

Jay was an Army reservist trained as a Blackhawk medevac pilot. After completing three tours in Iraq, he was well versed in getting people in and out of some very difficult places. On Jay's third deployment to Iraq, he was called on to fly two injured US personnel to safety.

When he landed at the site, one of the guys he was picking up had been assessed by the infantry medic and had a sheet covering his body. We had lost another one. KIA (killed in action). The other US soldier was being treated for wounds and prepped for takeoff. Ten minutes on the ground between landing and takeoff is not unusual for a medevac transport. Time is of the essence in this "golden hour." During these minutes, Jay sat there, staring at the form lying under the sheet. . . another one of our guys killed by the insurgency.

Tick, tick, tick. Jay turned toward his medics on the ground frantically working on the other patient to get him stabilized for flight. "It's time," he yelled. "We have to move. Let's go." He knew the longer they were on the ground, the less chance the remaining Alpha had of making it.

When the wounded soldier was finally prepped and ready to go, the company medic on the ground gave the thumbs up. Then he shouted a request over the whirling blades as they picked up speed in preparation for takeoff, "Hey can you guys take the deceased? It's going to be another two weeks in route to Tikrit, and I really don't want this guy traveling with us. It's hard enough for them to know he died but carrying his body for that long is going to be too much."

It was certainly a reasonable request given the circumstance. One small problem: Rules of Engagement (ROE). The ROE at the time stated that medevac Blackhawks were not allowed to transport KIA. In a hurry, Jay, the man who had to make the ultimate decision, agreed that transporting him was a command decision, and they would oblige the request. "Put him on, let's hurry," Jay said. Time was slipping away.

As a trained medic and pilot, it was his job and that of his crew to do whatever they could to ensure people got the best medical transport in the world en route to more advanced care. They risk life and limb to get our guys out of harm's way. They will put their own lives on the line for those who have been hurt in battle. And why do they do it? Because they would want someone to do it for them. We leave no one behind. No one!

Our medical care and training is the best in the world. We have over a 91% viability rate. If we can get our guys to a trauma level 1, often called a Role 3, they have a 91% chance of surviving. Those are better statistics than any war we have ever been in. Even with the devastating effects of IEDs, these guys do their best to defeat death. They are our nation's medical heroes.

In flight, there is a lot of chaos. It is extremely loud, people are trying to kill you, and you are trying to stabilize your patient, all while flying through a war zone. You are up against shock. Just trying to get a needle into a person can require drilling into bone. There is blood everywhere, tourniquets – you name it. The medics work fast and furiously, doing everything they can to defeat death. And more times than not, they succeed. And it is rewarding work. You can imagine the training it requires. It's hard enough to put in an IV line when a person is sitting or lying in front of you, on the ground, not moving. It's a completely different thing when you are flying at 160mph in a Blackhawk helicopter, in a war zone, being shot at and dodging bullets from small arms fire coming from the ground.

The extreme training is not limited to the medic. In addition to being trained to fly in very difficult conditions, the pilot also has extensive medical training. They are most likely the Senior Ranking Officer (SRO). They are the ones responsible for making decisions that affect people's lives. They decide if taking chances to get to our wounded is worth the risk. But they are not risk adverse. They will risk all to increase the chances that our guys live, all while trying to mitigate the risk to their crew and to themselves. They have to make tough decisions, and they make them every day.

And then it happened.

In flight, through all the chaos and craziness, they saw it. I have no idea how, but they did. One of the medics in the back over his radio said, "Did you just see that?" The pilot and other medic paused and went into autopilot mode, just long enough to see what would happen next. Thirty seconds went by, a lifetime in these circumstances. Nothing. Sometimes your mind plays tricks on you at times like this.

Flying a helicopter in a war zone is hard enough, let alone trying to focus in on everything that is happening. Did both medics have their eyes play tricks on them? Was it just the wind? No, it couldn't be. They had way too much training for that to occur, let alone for it to happen to both of them at the same time.

The medic feverishly returned to working on the injured, all the while trying desperately to reassure himself that he hadn't seen what he thought he'd seen. "There must be another answer," he told himself, constantly checking out of the corner of his eye for any sign.

Jay, the pilot, focused on flying, but his skills are such that he, too, was on autopilot. When so much information is flooding our brain in moments like these, we have the capability to inhibit over 95% of all stimuli. Jay's training makes him super focused, and yet there was that five percent of his brain that was now very attuned to both flying and to what he thought he saw.

After experiencing a very interesting 30 seconds, Jay said over the headset, "Okay, that was weird." They curtailed their checking, and Jay concentrated on flying while the flight medic continued to bag the wounded soldier with oxygen, desperately trying to keep him alive. "Just a few more minutes, and we will be at the Role 3," Jay reported. "Keep...." And in mid-sentence, it happened again.

The KIA moved. "He moved again, he moved. That guy just moved his leg. The KIA is alive!"

The guy with the sheet over him, the one purported to be KIA, was not. He was alive and struggling to survive. He needed immediate medical care. "Damn it, this guy is alive. How the hell did this happen?" Jay yelled in the frustrated voice of the guy who takes full responsibility for all that are on his Bird. "We've got to get him to the Role 3!"

Jay radioed ahead in a commanding, frustrated and almost panicked voice that you seldom hear from a trained and seasoned pilot. "Two Alphas en route! Not one Alpha, I repeat, we have *two* Alphas."

"Three Mikes, we're at three Mikes," Jay told air traffic control and the Tactical Operation Center.

"We've got two Alphas coming in?" the trauma surgeon asked.

"Roger that sir, not one but two Alphas."

The trauma team, hyper-focused themselves, changed the number under Alpha on the white board from a "1" to a "2." They wiped away the "1" under KIA.

"Let's get ready for two," the trauma surgeon said calmly as the team prepared for the wounded.

Three minutes is a long time in the air. "We could have been giving this guy medical attention 20 minutes ago, but he was labeled KIA. How the hell did this happen?" are the thoughts that ran through Jay's mind. "It's my responsibility to make sure this guy had no heartbeat. It is my job to verify this. We were sitting there for ten minutes, and I did nothing. I could have easily verified that this guy was dead. How did I not do my job?"

Remember that intense sense of responsibility we carry? The one where we take it personally when something goes wrong? In this case, someone had indicated one person was KIA, but Jay could have easily done what we in the military are repeatedly taught: Trust with Verification. We trust others, but we verify what they have said. In his mind, he had broken a major rule.

Jay's mind raced. "I didn't verify. I had time and sat there. I did nothing. I am a medic, and I just sat there and stared at that white sheet, assuming he was KIA when, in reality, he was fighting for his life. And I did nothing to help. Nothing."

"Blackhawk 424, preparing to land," Jay's voice was strong and forceful. "Two Alphas, I repeat *two* Alphas. Let's get these guys in there now!"

Within three minutes, the Blackhawk was on the ground, and the medical teams were running toward the bird. They all know their jobs and do them with precision. The two Alphas were taken off and immediately on their way to the trauma bay at the Role 3. During the short drive in the ambulance, every precaution is taken to increase their chances of survival. We spare no expense. We are highly trained personnel skilled beyond choreography. It is all part of the strategic plan to keep our guys alive. We have a brotherly love that goes beyond anything you can explain. And we will sacrifice anything to keep each other alive.

The Blackhawk, its blades whipping the air, waited for clearance from the medics on the ground. Jay moved his bird out of the landing zone in case others needed it for other medevac'd patients. While he waited for clearance, he took a brief moment to stare into space. Jay was experiencing the thousand-yard stare. How could this have happened? He blamed himself for not exiting the aircraft, for not checking on the deceased, for trusting but not verifying. "How did that happen? How could I have made such a huge mistake? What if this guy doesn't make it?" These are the thoughts that ran in a continuous stream through his mind as he stared off into oblivion.

But he had to move on. There were other injured personnel, other aircraft that needed that coveted space. Jay regained his situational awareness and got the thumbs up. He tried to clear his head and proceed to refuel. Jay knew that people got killed or injured when they lost focus, so he did his best to focus on the tasks at hand and not think about anything else. But it is hard, very hard, to just "let it go."

Jay had played sports as a kid, and his particular enjoyment was baseball. Out of nowhere he heard his dad's voice, "Let it go Jay, let it go." With tears in his eyes (which made it even more difficult to fly), Jay remembered his father's words as if they were spoken yesterday, even though he hadn't heard them for 15 years. As a small child, Jay had a really hard time forgetting about his "mistakes" and moving on. He would dwell on the play he had "errored" and would get super focused on what he had done wrong. It was the same characteristic that made him a great pilot. Super focused. And yet in that moment, this quality was working against him. He couldn't let it go. But he knew had to.

"I have a job to do," he told himself. He pictured his dad standing there, baseball in hand, bending over and handing it to him when he was the pitcher, then tapping him on the head and saying, "Let it go Jay, let it go." Jay felt as if he were that little boy again, reliving his life and wondering if he could do it. It was one thing in a game of baseball, but war, war was different. Jay glanced at the fuel tanks. "I have to let it go," he told himself. "Just let it go, Jay, let it go."

THE DEBRIEFING

Debriefings. We do them to find out what works and what doesn't work. We do them constantly. Why? Because it matters. In a combat zone, time is crucial. And the "golden hour" is never that – it's usually just minutes. And every minute is precious; every second counts.

Later, Jay called on the radio to get the report on the two Alphas they had dropped off. He heard someone say, "One Alpha is critical but stable," and then the radio went silent. Jay waited, but there

45

was no further transmission. His ears strained to hear even the slightest sound, and his heart sank.

"And the other one?" he finally asked.

"We're sorry, Tornado (his call sign). He expired."

Not knowing the situation, the flight surgeon added, "If only we had gotten to him a few minutes earlier, he might have survived. We were so close."

And there sat Jay, Blackhawk still whirling on the tarmac, waiting for the next call. He once again stared off into space thinking, "Just a few minutes earlier...just a few minutes earlier."

We have a tendency to repeat mantras – things we have concluded, things that matter. Just like the guy at the USO who repeatedly wondered, "Is this my last step? Is this my last step? Is this my last step?" It's what happens in war. We question our abilities. We question our decisions. We question ourselves.

We try to mitigate it as best we can. We try to stop death at all costs. But death continually rears its ugly head and claims another one in this fight against terrorism. And this was one we might have been able to steal from death's evil jaw, yet we did not. We did not verify; we did not check.

He might have made it, and yet we did not do what we are trained to do. We failed. And so we begin to listen to those "internal voices" and draw conclusions, "I failed. It was my responsibility. I should have verified that the information was correct. I know better." And the frustration and anger builds.

Our training makes it clear: medics in their unit are not to make those determinations. They are too close to the situation. "It was my responsibility to verify. I assumed they were correct. I assumed the white sheet was the tell-tale sign. I assumed they were KIA," and the thoughts do not stop. In reality, those thoughts can spin out of control. We repeatedly go around and around in our head, trying to make sense of what happened, what we did, what we could have done differently, all to change the outcome.

And so we do not think about the 99 out of 100 who lived, but instead, we beat ourselves up about the one who did not. We are haunted by our "failures," those times when we could not stop people from dying in war. Sure, we know it is war and that people die, but our job is not to let that happen. We think, "If only I had done something different, that person might still be alive." We repeatedly and methodically go over and over in our heads what we could or should have done differently. It's like watching game film on Monday morning as a quarterback, wondering how in the world we didn't see the cornerback who cut in front of the receiver and intercepted the ball. We go over and over and over it in our minds because this is much more than a game, it is people's lives. And our questioning of ourselves does not stop when our shift is over. The thoughts are relentless. We question ourselves and our actions time and time again. We keep asking ourselves those "what if" questions, and we relive what we did and didn't do. Why? Because we are human, and we are trained to take responsibility.

If you were Jay, what would you say to yourself? How would you "resolve" this issue? Would you blame yourself? Would you beat yourself up? What thoughts would ruminate in your mind? And when would it stop? When would you find relief? How would it come?

These are the haunting effects not of fear-based trauma, but of guilt-based trauma. This is about the guilt of inaction or omission – of "failure." We didn't do something that we could have done. This is a different kind of trauma than that suffered by rape victims and other victims of crime or violence. This is military trauma, and to resolve and heal this kind of trauma, we need a very different approach. We need an approach that specifically addresses survivor guilt, moral injury, guilt, and loss.

Jay needs answers because without them, he will relive this moment in his life a thousand times. He will question himself and lose sleep and re-experience it again and again. He will question his motives and his actions. And these thoughts will not stop. We often want an answer to the "why" questions. "Why did it have to happen?" "Why didn't I verify?" "Why couldn't we have gotten there three minutes earlier?"

Jay heard his dad's voice one more time: "Let it go, Jay, let it go."

CHAPTER 6: SURVIVOR GUILT

Survivor guilt occurs when a person survives a traumatic experience where others died or were seriously injured. The survivors often wonder why they were spared. The word wonder could be replaced by "haunted" or a myriad of other descriptive words. They may replay the event over and over in their mind, trying to make sense of it all. They might question whether they made the right decision, but mostly whether the outcome would have been different had they done something differently.

There are two basic types of decisions: decisions by omission and decisions by commission.

1. In decisions by omission, people *did not* make a decision which created detrimental consequences.
2. In decisions by commission, people *made* decisions which:
   a. directly created detrimental consequences, or
   b. accidently had detrimental consequences.

It's easy to play Monday morning quarterback *after* you know what happened. What is not possible is to go back to Sunday and change the outcome – no matter how strong your desire to do so.

Remember the two rules of war:

Rule #1: People die in war.

Rule #2: You can't change Rule #1.

No matter how hard we try, the reality is that we cannot change reality. What *has* happened will not change. That does not mean we do not try to learn from situations. Part of life is the continual assessment and re-assessment of our role in outcomes. Whether we are trained to do this formally or informally, it can either help or hinder. It can help in ensuring that, if we are put in the same or similar circumstances, we will not respond in the same way, thus, hopefully, creating a different outcome. Or it can hinder in that we can end up in an endless loop of trying to resolve a situation in which there seems to be no good outcome. We may even beat ourselves up for the decisions of omission or commission.

Most often, people who struggle with survivor guilt cannot help but ask themselves the "What if..." questions.

- "What if I had not taken that route?"
- "What if command had listened to us?"
- "What if I had just gone with my gut instinct?"
- "What if I had volunteered to go first?"
- "What if I hadn't left my men when I got injured?"
- "What if we hadn't been here in the first place?"
- "What if we weren't even in this war?"

The questions do not stop.

I explain to military members that there is actually one exemption to the two rules of war. All you have to be is:

1. Omniscient[9]
2. Omnipresent[10]
3. Omnipotent[11]

If a person is all three, he or she can actually mitigate rules #1 and #2 because at that point, the person would be all knowing, all present, and all powerful. It requires all three to mitigate bad outcomes in life. Know anyone who has all three? By definition, it would have to be God. Unfortunately, we are not Him, for if we

---

[9] All knowing
[10] Always present
[11] All powerful

were, we would have no need for war. Try as we might, we are human, and we want to control outcomes. But they are not ours to decide. God not only says he controls the powers and rulers of this world; he also can change outcomes of war by simply changing the smallest details, even simple things like weather conditions. Just look at WWII as it was replete with examples.

Just for fun, can you imagine having two of the characteristics of God listed above, but not the third? For example, if you were omnipresent and omnipotent, you could change the outcome of some things. But without omniscience, you wouldn't have the ability to know what the consequences would be ahead of time. Let's just say I'm glad God has all three. The idea of being omniscient will be a key factor as we begin to unfold this concept of God and Trauma.

Having the ability to know and see everything ahead of time, and even being able to know what is in a person's heart, or in a person's mind, before they even think it is crucial to God's ability to intervene with his mighty right hand (omnipotent). And because God can be everywhere all the time, the consequences of all three characteristics make it impossible for anything to ever surprise Him.

Even attempting to comprehend these three concepts changes how we will look at God's interventions in this world. But since we can't control God, and based on the fact that he decides what He will do on His end, let's look at things from our perspective and why it is we end up where we do.

THE INFLUENCE OF FEELING RESPONSIBLE

One of the biggest challenges we as military members face is the issue of responsibility. We are trained from boot camp on that we are responsible for the person next to us. It is ingrained in us to "leave no one behind," and to "bring everyone home alive." We even make promises to the family members of those who deploy with us that we will do whatever is necessary to get everyone home safe and sound. And why do we do this?

1. First, because that is our intent. We want it to be true.
2. Second, we want to give assurances that the people we deploy with will come home.
3. Third, we want to decrease anxiety. It's a natural human emotion. Unfortunately, we cannot always control what happens.

There are numerous situations over which we have no control. Remember Rule #1: people die in war. If one of our guys gets killed, we take it as a personal failure of responsibility. We believe that we have failed our mission and failed in bringing everyone home alive. This sense of responsibility is especially germane to US military personnel and those in our coalition forces.

REALIZATION THAT WE LACK POWER AND CONTROL

In the military, we are taught to follow orders without question. It is our job and responsibility to listen to senior officers and senior enlisted – in fact, it is in our commissioning oath. We have an obligation to follow command and to execute the orders of the President. Whatever the Commander-in-Chief decides, it is our job to execute those orders. What we often do not decide is the time, place, situation, assets, etc. "O" plans are designed to give us the best chance of winning a war, but anyone who has ever been in a firefight knows that the best plans are made and executed up until the first shot is fired.

It is not unusual for combat veterans to shift their strategy from a centralized plan of execution to a decentralized plan of execution. In other words, they make decisions based on what they see on the ground. This is not necessarily a bad thing because boots on the ground often have the best situational awareness. However, the problem lies in that the game plan may shift so fast on the battlefield, it's as if there is no game plan.[12] It becomes a battle of will and attrition. It is this attrition (death of a buddy) that haunts us.

To add to the complexity, the enemy has a voice in the matter and chooses their own time and place for such things as an ambush. And to make matters even worse, we may not always have all the equipment or personnel we need to accomplish the mission.

There are other confounding variables that can impact the battlefield. One, for example, is ROE. We had a situation where a particular country had a ROE that said they could not fire until fired upon. Insurgents were breaching our fence, and they could not fire at them. Why? Because they weren't being shot at! Even though the insurgents had explosives, they had not actually fired a shot. Fortunately, another country without that particular set of ROE rolled up in a Quick Reaction Force (QRF) and annihilated the insurgents. It was then that we decided to either ensure the first country change its ROEs or remove them from perimeter fence duty to avoid a similar incident. This kind of thing happens more often than not in a warzone.

In our assessment, we may conclude that there are numerous reasons why things turned out the way they did. If you have ever heard of Root Cause Analysis (RCA), this is trying to get at the root

---

[12] Those of you trained in John Boyd's OODA loop will understand this concept.

cause of why things happened the way they did. We try desperately to answer questions about the situation and why it happened. What we've listed here are but a few of the things that impact an outcome. Next, we will address the impact of what we bring to the table: our perspective and interpretations based on our core beliefs.

CHAPTER 7: FIVE CORE BELIEFS OF SURVIVOR GUILT AND MORAL INJURY

We want and need life to make sense. If it does not, we are often left feeling anxious or uncertain. It's as if there is a hole that needs to be filled. Blaise Pascal, the brilliant mathematician, claimed that there is a God-shaped vacuum in all of us that can only be filled by Him. Resolution to difficult questions in life is very much the same way.

The hole I'm talking about in the context of survivor guilt and moral injury is derived from cognitive dissonance and emotional lability. Cognitive dissonance is defined as two beliefs that compete with each other and are at odds, similar to a magnet where both positive poles attempt to occupy the same space. Emotional lability is when our emotions are difficult to control and are all over the place.

Both of these issues drive us to find answers. Although both concepts are difficult to comprehend, it all starts out when we are young with very basic core beliefs about ourselves, others, and the world around us.

At the heart of moral injury and survivor guilt are these core beliefs that start at a very young age.

1. We want what we want.

When we were kids, we were taught there was right and wrong. We were also taught what was acceptable behavior and what was not. Sometimes the very first word we learned was "No" because we heard it so often. As children, we pitted our behavior against what our parents wanted us to do. Our behavior seems to be innate. Let's start with a basic premise that goes to the heart of each us. Starting from early childhood, we are truly a little on the selfish side. We want what we want. How do I know this? Because another word we quickly learn as a child is "Mine!" How many times have you heard a kid repeat over and over, "mine, mine, mine"? Those of you who are parents know this stage all too well. You didn't teach it to your kids, they came by it naturally.

2. We want things to be fair.

When we as kids do not get what we want, especially when it is something we perceive is ours, what is the first thing we argue for? Fairness. Kids are often quick to say, "That's not fair!" especially when they perceive an injustice.

We didn't take a class on fairness in our mother's womb, and yet we are very, very eager to make our arguments for fairness.

Even as I write this, my wife and I struggle with our two boys, Joshua, age 11, and Peyton, age 10. They both want what they want. This creates arguments over fairness, sometimes all day long it seems. Joshua, being bigger, has at times chosen brute force to take what he wants. He has two inches and 30 pounds on Peyton. He can forcefully make Peyton do what he wants. Of course, Peyton then gets mad and either does something to get back at Joshua or figures out that if he asks my wife or me to intervene, we will make our best decision at the time, which often results in Peyton getting what he wants.

I wonder what it was like when you were growing up. Did you have similar issues? And which role did you play? Were you the older or the younger child (or the bigger or smaller one)? Did you have a brother or sister who took things from you, was "selfish" and unwilling to play fair? If you had a sibling, I can almost assure you that this was the case.

3. We want things to be just.

Have you ever noticed that when we perceive things to be unfair, our first reaction is to demand justice? It doesn't take much for us as children to go to our parents and make an argument that things are not fair and that they should do something about it. In essence, we want things to be fair, and if they are not, we want justice.

When we were young, if we had a toy that our brother or sister took from us, we either took it back or demanded that our parents get it for us. Why? Because "we had it first." If someone takes something from us, not only is it not fair, but we also want justice.

We quickly learn that if we try to take what we want by force, that behavior doesn't go over well. Also, most parents get to a point where they cannot stand the fighting and tell us to come to them for resolution. They will solve it. Eventually, we end up going to our parents for resolution. We learn to call on a higher authority to intervene when we cannot get what we want.

4. We want and need authority figures to intervene on our behalf.

Our parents are usually the first experience we have of an authority figure. We quickly learn that they have a lot of power and influence over us. What parents say goes, especially when you are dependent upon them for the basics of life. When one is dependent upon acting a certain way to get food, one usually acquiesces quickly. If you don't believe me, think about when you were an infant and nursing. If you bit your mom, you quickly found out that was unacceptable behavior. You either changed your behavior, or you didn't get fed!

Throughout our formative years, we learn that certain behavior elicits a certain response. If we act a certain way, we usually get a desired outcome, good or bad. This classical conditioning technique is repeated on a daily basis.

There is also a time when we believe that our parents are omniscient, omnipotent, and omnipresent. As a parent, it's an awesome feeling to think that you are a superhero and can do anything. Kids look up to their parents at a certain phase of life and are in awe of what they can do. They even believe moms have eyes in the backs of their heads and that's how they know everything. Well, at least that is what we tell them.

As time progresses, especially into our teenage years, we learn that our parents are not as omniscient, omnipotent, or omnipresent as we once thought. It is very normal for young people to begin to challenge their parents, not only physically (in things like wrestling) but also intellectually (as in thinking their parents are stupid).

Then reality starts to hit. Our core beliefs are refined. Sometimes life circumstances bring us to the conclusion that our parents cannot make certain things happen. No matter how much they may want to, they do not have the capability to control certain things. They either don't have enough money, time, or energy to make things happen that we want. Maybe you can think of something where this transition happened for you.

Also, school and church influences help formulate our core beliefs. For the context of this book, I want to focus on those of us who attended church and possibly Sunday School. We learned about God's characteristics. We learned that God is omniscient, omnipresent, and omnipotent. We are intrigued by the concept of God and how we came about in this world. We sometimes wonder why we were born and what our purpose in life is. And because our parents are limited in their abilities, we often look to God for those answers.

This leads us to another core belief: *our desire to find answers to life's questions brings us to the concept of God.* From a Judeo-Christian perspective, we are taught that God not only loves us unconditionally, but that He also has all authority and power.

When we cannot control life events, we want and need someone who can - someone who can intervene on our behalf and make things happen. Therefore, it is a natural progression to go from our earthly father to our heavenly father in this regard. For those of us who grew up with a dad, we know that they are big, and they are strong. They can also will things to happen with just their voice. God is very much the same. Only He can create the sun, earth, and stars by speaking them into being.

5. We often only see things from our perspective.

My son Joshua is a perfect example of this. When he was about three years old, he was convinced that he never slept. He would say, "No, daddy, I never sleep." Of course, he did, and he would be asleep and not know it, but trying to convince a three-year-old of that was another matter. I would even videotape him sleeping and show him the "evidence," but of course, he came up with an answer for that as well. He said, "Well, I was just resting my eyes." Finally, it was my wife who said to me, "David, give it up. You are trying to argue with a three-year-old." She was right, of course, but it didn't deter me from still trying. Don't even analyze how this battle of the minds is going to turn out when he is a teenager!

The point is this: sometimes trying to change a person's perspective is as difficult as trying to change a three-year old's mind about not sleeping. Joshua was entrenched in his belief system, and despite all evidence, he would argue that he never slept. And he was not going to change his mind.

So, to recap, what core beliefs do we hold at a young age?

1. We want what we want.
2. We want life to be fair.
3. We want things to be just.
4. We turn to authority figures for answers.
5. We often only see things from our perspective.

How do these five basic core beliefs have any impact on issues of moral injury and survivor guilt?

Childhood is a precursor to adulthood. We carry these core beliefs with us right into adulthood. Everything we learn about human behavior as a child is translated into a core belief system about ourselves, other people, and life events. Core beliefs help us not only to make sense of the world, but also to navigate it. Allow me to use a personal example of a real-life situation and the impact of core beliefs on cognitive dissonance.

CHAPTER 8: BAD NEWS IS NEVER BETTER LATER

It was a day I will never forget. My mom sat down with me and repeated the news she had received from her doctor, "I have breast cancer."

In my mind, there was no time to waste. I was working on my undergraduate degree at the time and was determined at all cost to finish my last year and get home to be with her. I took 24 credit hours my last semester and was able to complete my degree just as she was going into hospice.

Remember our core beliefs? The very first one? We want things to be fair. I felt that life wasn't fair. Why was it my mom who had to get cancer? Why not someone else? What did she do to deserve this horrible disease? Why did she have to suffer from the after-effects of chemotherapy, including losing her hair and being so fatigued she could barely walk or even go outside to listen to the birds sing?

Watching my mom slowly die created an incredible sadness inside me. That sadness was soon replaced by the hope that God would intervene. I hoped God's higher authority would make it right. In reality, what happened was that my hope began to fade with each day she went through chemotherapy and the dying process. I wanted justice (another core belief), and I wanted it now ("I want what I want," another core belief).

I had been brought up in church to believe in God and to respect Him. I was also taught that He loved me unconditionally and that He was always there for me, that when all else failed, God was always an ever-present help in times of trouble.

So where was God in the midst of my pain and suffering? Where was God while I watched my mom suffer from the cancer that was wreaking havoc on her body? You see, it was quite clear my two worlds were colliding. I had two belief systems that could not co-exist. My two negative, magnetic poles were in a fight with each other for the same space, and only one was going to win.

I wanted fairness. I wanted my mom to be healthy and her getting cancer wasn't fair. I also wanted what I wanted. I was being selfish, but I didn't care. I wanted my mom to be alive and to be there for me. Sure, call it selfishness, call it whatever you want, but call it over. Call cancer away from her body.

I remember being taught that people were healed not only by touching Jesus but also by His just saying the words. So, in my mind, why wouldn't He just say the words? And so began my attempts to invoke God. Say the words, God, just say them. Say, "Cancer, be gone," and it will be gone. Say the same words with the same power that you used to raise Lazarus from the dead. Say, "Come forth," and death must relinquish its grip. God almighty, you are all-powerful, you are mighty, you are God, and whatever you say goes. You know everything (omniscient) and know exactly where the cancer is in her body. And since you are all-powerful (omnipotent), the cancer must obey – so just tell it to go away. And so went my appeal to a higher authority for intervention (another core belief).

But God did not speak. He remained silent!

My mom and I both needed an all-powerful, all-knowing, and ever-present authority figure. And yet God made the decision not to act. But why? Was it something I did or didn't do? Was it something that my mom did or didn't do? What was it? Did I not have enough faith? Was this on my shoulders? Why was God not responding as I wanted Him to? Life was not being fair, and I wanted God to intervene, but from what I could "see," He chose to do nothing. And so began my struggle with God and his fairness and justice.

Maybe you have had similar experiences in your life when you wanted God to intervene and do what you desired; to say the word and change life's circumstances, to intervene in a way that only God can.

In my pleas for intervention, I was trying to resolve this tension between my belief in an all-powerful God who loves me and His unresponsiveness.

Where was God's mercy? He is, after all, the God of love and mercy. Of all of the characteristics we use to describe God, there are certain ones I needed in my life at that time. I wanted them. I...well, I demanded them.

You, too, may have been taught that God has certain characteristics. He is omniscient, omnipotent, and omnipresent. And He loves me. So, if God is all three and loves me, it only made sense that God would do as I asked. Why would He not heal my mom? Or why wouldn't He hear your prayers and stop your friend from getting killed? If He truly is who He says He is, He will do exactly what I want.

Growing up in a Christian home, I was taught that if you are good, you will get what you want. This behavior was reinforced over and over again. If you clean your room, you will get a reward. If your behavior is good in church, you will get ice cream for dessert. If you are nice to your brothers, you will get a toy.

So, it only made sense that the issue of goodness would come into play as I attempted to get God to do as I asked. Unfortunately, I had one small problem...I knew deep down I wasn't good. Or at least, I wasn't good enough.

ANCIENT HISTORY LESSON FROM ARCHERY

Back in the days of archery, there was a particular word that people called out when someone missed their target or mark. Any idea what the word was in ancient history?

Take a guess? _____

The word was "sin." They called out SIN anytime someone missed the mark.

This issue became very important because the ultimate question had to do with my core beliefs and whether or not I was good or good enough. Remember, all throughout childhood, we are often taught that if we are good or do good things, then good things will happen. So clearly, if I wanted my mom to live, I needed to be a good person. Unfortunately, I may be good, but I'm not perfect.

Back to the archery example. If you shot 100 arrows and missed even one, they would call out "sin," and you were disqualified from your perfect marksmanship. You know that one in the military where we get a badge for marksmanship? Over the course of time, there would be no one who could consistently hit the bullseye. No one. This is also why I am convinced that in Revelation there is none who was found worthy to unroll the scrolls except for one.[13] The perfect one. And I doubt that you or I, just like Joshua and his belief that he was right, could argue otherwise.

---

[13] Revelation 5: 1-7

I was relying on the concept of being good; therefore, God would do what I wanted. You see, there are so many basic core beliefs we hold that play out in survivor guilt and moral injury. Even the most basic one says, "If you are good, I will give you what you want." But if that were true, why wasn't God answering my prayers the way I wanted? It must be, I thought, because I am not good or can't hit the mark every time. Well, if that is the case, I will never be good enough.

Had I done something so egregious, even possibly unforgiveable, that God was not willing to hear my prayers? Was it because I had missed the mark, was imperfect, a sinner that He wouldn't listen? And even though I am not perfect, I do the best I can. So why, if God is so loving, would He simply not just do as I asked? And so it goes: *we appeal to a God we do not see to intervene in a way we cannot control.*

So, I continued my attempts to coerce God to intervene.

Please, God, are you not listening? Do you not care? Where is your right hand of justice and mercy? My mom is a beautiful, wonderful, giving person. There are plenty of people in this world who you could take instead. God, take me. Take me in her place.

Where are you in my time of need? Why do you not intervene? *God, are you there?*

In hindsight, all of my questions and core beliefs came down to this: I could only see answers to my questions being solved from my vantage point. God, give me what I want. And because of my own desires, all I wanted was what I wanted. It was time for God to intervene, and to do so on my terms. The only answer I wanted was for my mom to be healed. And God needed to make that happen. Period.

Let me just say that when we get to a point in our life that we are dictating to God how He should act, we are not only on shallow ground, we are on thin ice, about to be plunged into ice cold water.

In life, there is a bigger picture at work that we are sometimes blind to and cannot see. In order to grasp the enormity of what we are dealing with, we cannot be limited to just our own perspective. It is much too small and narrow. We instead must see a much bigger picture. Why? Because questions about the meaning of life, about why God does or does not intervene, about what our purpose on earth is, are not simple questions. They are questions that have to be answered on a much grander, broader scale.

No, we have to see this not from our limited perspective and what we want, but from God's perspective. When life doesn't go the way we want it to, it forces us to open the aperture of possibilities that there is more to life than just our perspective and what we want. In life, tragedy provides us with opportunity. And in this case, it is the opportunity to find answers that require a totally different perspective. In reality, what happens in trying to gain this perspective on life is that we are constantly pulled back by wanting what we want and not necessarily what God has in store.

FAIRNESS DEMANDS JUSTICE

We as humans feel we have the right to demand answers. When we are powerless over situations, we, like young children, look to answers from those who have the power to intervene. Why? Because we want there to be action. Sometimes we don't even care about anything other than what we want. Inherently, we are relational people who give and take love. And there is no other person in this world I loved more than my mom. And so, I made my pleas.

"God, you created her, and you gave me to her. So, God, since I cannot fix this, and you can, I'll do anything you want. Anything."

Time passed, and she continued to deteriorate. Elizabeth Kubler-Ross, a writer on grief and loss, created the five stages of coping with death and dying. The mnemonic is DABDA: Denial, Anger, Bargaining, Depression, Acceptance. A person can go in and out of each of them during different stages of the process. Personally, I often experience Bargaining prior to Anger. And it's usually when I feel things are not going my way that I resort to demands. I had done everything I could to cajole God to intervene. But ultimately, it became obvious that death was winning. At that point, my anger surfaced, "God, heal my mom! Now! Please! Just do it!" as I looked up to the sky and demanded action.

And why is it that we are so demanding at times like this? Because there is so much on the line. The consequences are too severe. Life is too fragile.

Even in our limited scope, we know we are not omnipotent. We do not have the power to change reality based on our will. But we do know who does. ***God is the only answer left to our dilemma.*** He is the only one who is omniscient, omnipotent and omnipresent. If we had those characteristics, we would do it ourselves. Let me repeat that. If we had the ability that God does, we would do it differently. We would use our power and authority over death. I would touch my mom, and she would be healed.

There is but one small problem. I don't have that power. By the way, neither do you.

But God does. And we go with what we know. We are powerless, but God is not.

IS GOD FAIR?

We typically do not question God's characteristics because to do so would mean all hope is lost. If we did not believe that God is all-powerful, all-knowing, and ever-present, then what kind of God is He after all? No, that would leave us with no one who can change the collision course we are on with death. And remember, our ultimate goal is to get what we want.

So, we cajole, we ask, we beg, we even promise to do whatever it takes to get God to answer our prayers the way we desire. Sometimes God does answer the way we wish, but there are times when He is silent. We hear nothing, see nothing. We often wonder how a God whom we have been taught is loving could leave us longing.

Over time, we take a deep heavy sigh and begin to slowly accept that God may not intervene. In essence, God is not doing what we want Him to do. Slowly, reality and our biggest fears come to fruition. And we begin to draw conclusions, conclusions that strike at our core beliefs. You know those voices inside of us that drive our behavior. The same voices that can bring about comfort can also bring about desperation. The slippery slope can go from desperation to depression to despair to death. And so we draw our conclusions over time, based on what we see, on the reality that is before us.

Maybe God is not fair. Maybe God doesn't love me. Heavy sigh... Maybe God is not even God.

I have seen it many times. God does not do what we want or ask, so we conclude God either doesn't care about us, doesn't love us, or simply isn't real. Why? Because we cannot fathom that someone whom we have been taught loves us unconditionally would let this happen to us. You see, God, all of this is about us anyway. We want what we want. And because you are God, GIVE ME WHAT I WANT.

Remember when I said it started in childhood? Is it starting to sound familiar? We want what we want, and we want it now. So, give it to me. Please heal my mom.

Honestly, in our pain and suffering, we feel this is not an unreasonable request. It is, after all, a simple one. One that wouldn't take much of your time, God. Just two words, "Be healed," and it will happen. I trust in you, and I know you can do it. Maybe just one word, God: "Cured." Can you spare just that one word, that one simple word, God? Are you listening? Where are you? Are you there, God? And so this process of negotiation and appealing to His grace and mercy continues.

COGNITIVE DISSONANCE

We have now set up an internal fight between what we believe and what we experience in real life. This is the essence of what psychologists call cognitive dissonance – two conflicting beliefs crashing into each other, two beliefs that we firmly hold to be true but no longer seem to fit together. To hold one means to have to get rid of the other. They cannot logically coexist. God loves me, but God will not intervene. God has power over death but will not cure my mom. God is God, and I am not, but He won't do what I ask. Remember, God, you were the one who said, "Ask, and it shall be given unto you." Well, God, I'm asking.

But you are not responding, God. We are clear: you are God, and I am not, so please *do as I ask.*

And then she died.

CHAPTER 9: THE PROCESS OF DECIDING WHAT ONE BELIEVES

O ur humanity and everything inside of us begins to crack at our core and has the potential to fall apart from the inside out. It's like a volcanic eruption of the soul or what others may term "an emotional breakdown." The intensity can be so overwhelming that I literally tell people that it builds and builds and builds to the point our emotions pour out our eyeballs. We take a deep breath in, our shoulders shrug down, and with a thud of the heart, mind and soul, we surrender to our fate. And so, with a heavy sigh and enough tears shed to fill any lake, we can be left feeling as if God is powerless, or God does not care, or even worse, that God does not love us.

Why do we feel this way? Because when we asked, God did not intervene. And so we chisel away at our two competing beliefs that no longer fit together. It's like two semi-trucks that want to occupy the same space on a bridge. In physics, it is called the Pauli exclusion principle. A crude definition is this: two or more particles cannot occupy the same space at the same time. The laws of physics which God created do not change. The law will not relent. Something must give. One of these particles is going to get shattered. So is one of my beliefs.

Maybe, just maybe, my belief is in something that doesn't even exist. Maybe there is no God. Maybe this is all a farce. Maybe God is not real. Maybe, just maybe, atheists have it right. And so here comes a new, refined mantra based on my experience: "It's not that God doesn't love me. It's that God isn't real."

Let that statement sink in, just as it does for someone who experiences it. "It's not that God doesn't love me. It's that God isn't real."

When it comes to cognitive dissonance, we often take the path of least resistance. You see, it's just easier.[14] Believing that "God is dead," as the front page of *Time* magazine once declared, or that "He doesn't exist" is much easier to tolerate than believing that God doesn't love us. We need to feel loved. We were created to give and receive love. To be rejected by the one who made us, who created us, who gave us our life's breath, that is intolerable.

In the deepest recesses of our soul, we cannot live with the feeling we are not loved by a loving God. We cannot handle or accept that that is true. In our finite mind, we are left with two competing beliefs, and one of them must give way. The trucks are not only headed at each other, but they have now also smashed into each other. There is debris everywhere. The impact, the smashing of metal into metal, the reverberation, the fire, the feeling one would experience if they were in the driver seat can be, well, deadly. Soul eruption is real. And we are left with either one of two beliefs: either God isn't real, or He doesn't love us. Which would you choose?

This is where core beliefs can be forever altered.

---

[14] From Mike Hauser, Licensed Professional Counselor: "Humans abhor a void, so we fill in the blanks in our understanding. Something I often run into with vets is that they fill in the blank with false information because that is preferable to doing the hard work of understanding complex or complicated subjects. But living with the misinformation actually creates its own problems."

What many conclude is that God is not real. In the end, it is not that God cannot or does not love me; it is that He simply doesn't exist. *That* reality I can handle. I can tolerate and accept it. I don't like it, but it's better than believing God doesn't care about me and that I've been rejected. God not loving me is something I cannot, nor will ever, accept. Therefore, I conclude, there is no God.

ANGER AT GOD

Even as we try to resolve our belief or non-belief in God, we get angry. Remember the two trucks colliding? The heat that is generated is similar to our anger. I believe it is actually more than anger, it's rage. Combat veterans don't have an anger problem, we have a rage problem. You should see what really goes on inside of us. If it weren't for our frontal lobe where we stop ourselves, you would really see the raw emotion and intensity of which we live. And to be honest, we don't want you to see that side of us. It's another piece of us that has been altered by war.

Instead, we want what we want, but we cannot have it. Reality dictates that we cannot have it both ways. If God is dead, there is no alternative or answer to many questions, let alone our wants and needs to be addressed. Where are we to turn?[15] The eruption of our soul is like heartburn that without treatment will destroy our

---

[15] Toward the end of His life, Jesus started to challenge His disciples so that they would begin to understand more complex issues. Many of His disciples left Him because His teachings were too difficult, and the teachings were not what they wanted to hear. So, Jesus asked the 12 who remained, "Does this offend you?" and later He said, "You do not want to leave, too, do you?" Peter (the impulsive one) said, in response, something truer than he could imagine at the time, "Lord, to whom shall we go?" This story can be found in John 6:61-69. It points to the impossible position we find ourselves in if God does not exist.

esophagus. It burns, and it keeps us up at night. Although we try as hard as we might, we have to get out of bed and find an answer because no matter what, that burning sensation will not remit, and we will not find comfort or peace.

Our anger is much the same as heartburn. If left unresolved, it eats at us, burns and eventually explodes. And why is that again? Because at our core, we cannot fathom a God – if there even is a God – who does not love us.[16] And not only does He not love us, but He also won't grant us one humble request. God will not give us what we want, and he is not being fair.

We cannot fathom why a God who has perfect characteristics, and is perfect Himself, would not do what we ask and heal someone we love.

Time passes, and we go on with our lives and our attempts at solving our cognitive dissonance.

Enter stage right years later when we are now in military service and find ourselves in a warzone. Remember, our process of deciding what we believe is altered throughout life based on our experiences. Reality has a way of changing our perspective and our beliefs.

RE-EVALUATING CORE BELIEFS

When our parents are gone along with our emotional safety net, it is our turn to be the adult. Instead of the voices from our parents being heard audibly, it is our own voices that we are left with. When we see evil staring straight at us in a warzone, when we face atrocities that no one should ever see, we revert to our previous belief systems and conclusions. When we see the consequences of

[16] Perhaps, even worse would be a God who doesn't care, or maybe even dislikes us, actively resisting and frustrating our plans.

war, we may once again wonder if there is more to life than death, we may even re-ponder the whole concept of God. Even though, because of our previous experiences, we may have determined there is no God, we now question the accuracy of our conclusion. And we wonder, just because we've decided that God is not real, does that make it true? Did God disappear just because we no longer believe in him? Is our cognitive dilemma resolved?

The whole concept of God is inherently confusing when we have beliefs that are in direct opposition to what we see and experience. But God is not only a God of love, He is also a God of mercy and hope. And sometimes we need hope more than we need air. We need to believe that there is more to life than just death and destruction.

I had a fellow veteran share this perspective with me:

"I have come to understand that the human experience inherent to a combat veteran is one marked by contrast. In one breath, we witness firsthand the comforts of peace and blessings of prosperity. In the next breath, we witness in graphic detail the tragedy of war and widespread poverty. This is the great dualism of life and circumstance. By the very nature of our inherent duties, we are, by the hands of our Creator, taught that life is both precious and painful. The joy we experience during the birth of a child contrasted against the pain associated with the loss of a loved one. It is profound and yet all so necessary. How would we recognize good if there was no evil? How would we come to appreciate light if there was no darkness? How would we come to appreciate life if there was no death? This is life...and the purpose of life, in my humble opinion, is to do good, to alleviate suffering, to share hope, to know the virtue of love and to seek truth. I believe we will be changed men and women every day if we choose to awaken each morning as our Creator's students and realize that life...is His classroom."[17]

You can see how this former military member has altered his belief system to a place where he has found solitude. He no longer struggles with cognitive dissonance. Resolution is a significant key to resilience.

Have you resolved your internal conflicts? *Where are you in this process?* What adjectives would you currently use to describe God? List those in your head, or write them down. Either way, they will be very telling.

The characteristics I ascribe to God are:

_____

_____

_____

_____

GOD IN WAR

We see and experience things in war people should not have to experience. No wonder God said, "Thou shalt not kill."[18] Killing is horrible. People are not meant to kill other people. Life is too fragile. The people we kill may be our enemy, but they are also human. And what are we fighting for in the first place? Oftentimes it is one leader who wants what another leader has. A king or a president or a monarch says, "That is mine. I want it." And the other person says, "If you want it, you'll have to come and take it."

---

[17] Sammy Villela (2017)
[18] The actual meaning of "kill" in the Bible is murder.

And so it goes. Remember back to childhood. I want what I want, and you have it, so give it to me or else.

When you ask a military member what chess piece they relate to on a chess board, they almost inevitably say the same piece - a pawn. And why is that? Pawns have two characteristics. First, they have very little power. Second, they are expendable. Most of us, no matter our rank in the military, feel we are both. And the closer we are to war, the closer we are to killing insurgents, the closer we are to knocking down doors, the closer we are to death.

We are not only powerless and pawns, but we also see and experience evil and death up close and personal – sometimes so close it is right next to us.

We combine our sense of responsibility to bring everyone home alive with the reality that there are people who are dead set on killing us and making sure that does not happen. And sometimes they succeed. A pawn is removed from the game: a brother or sister who was fighting right next to us is killed by an IED, sniper fire, RPG, Chinese 107 rocket or any number of other ways. And we, we are spared. We survive, but why? Why did they have to die when they have a family and kids and a future? Why was it that they died instead of us? It is not fair for them to die and for me to live. Once again, we begin asking questions based on our perception of what is fair.

We are not worthy, we are not special – and we, too, are a pawn that could just as easily have been taken off the board. Was it fate that they died, and we lived? And for what possible reason? Why are we alive? Was it by chance that we were spared, or is there a bigger purpose or plan at work? And just like that, we are back to questioning our core beliefs and dealing with our cognitive dissonance.

We are left pondering life and death questions and wondering why God did or did not intervene.

Even over time, the questions do not stop. "Why am I alive? Why was I spared and my buddy killed? Is there a purpose behind my being left behind? If so, what is it?

If you think time heals, it doesn't. If it did, every WWII, Korea, and Vietnam veteran would simply have no cognitive dissonance. God knows they have endured enough time. So, we flash back to our earlier conclusions and how we attempted to resolve them. And as any normal human does, we begin to question ourselves. Were my conclusions correct? Is God dead? If there is no God, is there any hope? What if I am wrong? What if God is alive, and there is another answer to all of this craziness? And the "what if" questions keep coming to the forefront of our mind.

You see, we appeal to a God we cannot see because we so desperately want and need justice to exist. What we experience in life cannot be for naught. There is a right and a wrong, and even if we do not get justice in this life, we hope and pray that there is a God who, in the end, will make it right. When we think people have gotten away with things, we want to believe in an authority figure who will make it right. And sometimes that means bringing people to justice. Deep down inside, we believe in the Navy Seal statement that goes something like this: "God will judge our enemies. We'll arrange the meeting."

We want a God who is fair and right and just. But when we don't see it happening in this life, we begin to expand our perceptions of when justice may occur.

Maybe this life is just a precursor to the afterlife. Maybe this is just a test. Maybe God is a God who *will*, in the end, make it right. Maybe the spirit inside us continues on and to be "apart from the body is to be with the Lord" really is true. Maybe I had it all wrong because I was so angry that God didn't do what I wanted. Maybe my mom is alive in heaven, and one day I will see her again. Maybe, just maybe, this is all a test to see how I will handle life's reality, especially when I don't get what I want.

FREE WILL

What if God loves us so much that He gives us free will at any cost? And with that free will comes the freedom to choose what we believe, how we act, and what we do. Maybe, just maybe, God loves us so much that He chooses to let us make our own decisions. And sometimes, kings and rulers use their free will in a way that impacts the rest of us.

We joined the military to protect and defend the constitution of the United States from enemies both foreign and domestic. Maybe God lets free will reign at all cost. Maybe this isn't God's choosing so much as He decreed, "Okay, you want to decide, so be it. The choice is yours, but so are the consequences." It wouldn't be the first time that he said, "Okay, you want a king? I'll give you a king."[19]

I'm not sure if you've gotten to the point in life that you wish you didn't have free will, but I have. I also wish that others didn't have it. I wish we could just go back and do it God's way. I wonder at times what life would have been like had Adam and Eve not sinned. I wonder if we would even have war at all. I wonder what the Garden of Eden would be like today? Is it possible that the

---

[19] In 1 Samuel 8, the Israelites demanded a king, just like the neighboring countries. Until that point, God was the leader of the nation. The request for a human king was considered by God to be a rejection of Himself. So, He gave the nation a human king, then sent Samuel to warn them they would suffer under human leadership. This is an example of "be careful what you ask for." In the short term, it may seem like a good decision, but the long-term consequences may not turn out to be what you had hoped.

world, and the wars that we live with, could be the result of humans exercising their free will?

You have undoubtedly noticed in my writing that I am once again dealing with my own cognitive dissonance issues. It's a process, not just for me, but probably for you as well. As for me, I'm trying to find ultimate resolution. I need answers that work for me; answers that make sense of the world. I want to know that there is ultimate fairness and justice. And maybe you and I are not too far apart in that way? What do you do with these questions? What questions do you ask? Where are you in this process?

Maybe, just maybe, God is not only real but is taking notes. You see, God's character and His nature, by definition, will bring about justice. Throughout scripture, we see God at work, testing people. All one has to do is look at the example of Job. Most people know of the story of Job, even to the point that his wife encouraged him to just "curse God and die." It was that bad. And yet, God allowed all of this misery to come upon him, a righteous man whose life was destroyed – his home and wealth taken, his sons killed, his body afflicted to the point of experiencing boils all over his body. He would even sit with clothes torn in ashes as a sign of suffering, all while scraping himself to find relief. And what did Job do to deserve this? Nothing.

So why in the world would God allow such a thing to happen to such a righteous man? Because God wanted us to learn a very important lesson from Job, just like He does with most of the stories in the scriptures. It may be hard for us to reach our brains around this concept, but God foreknew what Job would do. He knew what Job would decide. God decided to let it play out so that Job would know. But what about you? What will you do? God already knows that answer as well. But you get to decide, which is the irony. You see, God takes "notes" not for His sake, but for ours. Justice will occur one way or the other. Sometimes we want to be the one to bring the justice, to take matters into our own hands. It's that Navy Seals saying again, "It's God's job to judge; it's our job to arrange the meeting." When things happen to us that are beyond egregious, our sense of justice gets triggered, and we want revenge. It's natural for that to happen.

But God, God has a different way, a different plan. You see, God knows the heart. We do not. That is why I am convinced that He says, "revenge is mine sayeth the Lord, I will repay." We are quick to demand justice when we are the ones who have been offended. But when we are the culprit, we want grace. That's another reason why I believe God says, "forgive and you will be forgiven." It is true that God is a God of justice, and He is the only one who can truly understand and differentiate the human heart. As for the question of what a person should receive - justice or mercy? – well, I would speculate it depends on which side of the coin you are on. Again, we want and demand justice for injustice, but when it is us who has offended or "sinned," we hope and pray for mercy. Even though most of us have never experienced it, I doubt anyone would ever want to experience God's wrath. Or, at least if they were smart, they wouldn't. And who better to make the decision of justice and/or mercy than the one who created all of humanity? God himself.

You see, I want and need a God who will ultimately make all things right. I need it for my own cognitive dissonance. I need resolution, and I need answers. I think that is ultimately what people who experience survivor guilt want – answers. They want answers to questions that only an omniscient, omnipotent, and omnipresent God can give. But God does not work on our timetable, and we cannot be demanding or even coerce Him to speak or act. When persecuted before the Roman authorities of the day, Jesus remained silent.[20]

If God were to speak, there would be no need for faith. Faith, by definition, is believing in something you cannot prove. If believing in God requires faith, well, it is definitely a choice because we have to make decisions about what we believe in. If God were to speak, it might raise questions about our psychological stability because we would question whether or not we truly heard His voice, but we would definitely not need faith.

Maybe it is true that this life is just a test[21] and that, in heaven, we will receive our rewards for what we have done while on earth – good or bad. Maybe there *is* a God who sees that which we do in secret and will reward accordingly. Note that I say, "in secret," not those who stand up and say, "Look at me! Look at the good I am doing." Instead, maybe it's true that God gives grace to the humble.

Wherever you are in this process, and it is a process, you have to resolve things in *your* mind. Cognitive dissonance not only does not work for us, but it also haunts us. It keeps us up at night. You may not know this, but the defense mechanisms we use in the daytime are not present at night. They cease to exist. And this is why we struggle at night trying to find resolution. So when we go up against evil and an unjust world, we look to the one who has all the authority and power to make it right. And rightfully so.

And who are we anyway to question God? What power, what authority, what right do we have? Where were we when God created the world? Where were we when He separated the oceans from land? Where were we when He created the sun, the earth, the moon and the stars? Where were we when He was willing to allow His son

---

[20] There are at least 14 references in the Bible wherein Jesus was given opportunity to speak, to defend Himself, yet He chose to remain silent, even when He knew that the result would be His own death.

[21] The Bible makes a distinction between "*testing*" and "*tempting*." God tested Abraham. And He allows humans to be tempted, but He does not put temptation before anyone. See James 1:13.

to die on a cross to give all of humanity an answer? We were not even yet created. We did not even exist. We had not yet been spoken into being. So, who are we to question God and his motives?

WE ARE HUMAN, AND THAT IS WHY WE STRUGGLE

We struggle with the reality of this world, especially when it does not make sense to us. We want God to do what only God can do: intervene and make it right. Why? Because we are finite and human, and He is infinite and God. We are not omniscient, omnipotent, and omnipresent, so we want Him to intervene. We want Him to stop cancer, and we want Him to intervene when one of our buddies gets killed in a firefight. But we also understand that He may not. It's not that He is powerless. It's not that He doesn't care. It's not that He is incapable. Quite the opposite. God made the decision to give humans free will and the ability to choose. God is willing to let humans decide. You see, God can do all of that and at times has. All one has to do is look at the book of Acts. And yet, the same is also true that at times He does not choose to intervene. Trying to resolve and make sense of this is our exact cognitive dissonance issue that creates our belief system and our place in this world. In my own resolution, I have concluded that it is our free will that is the cause of a lot of pain and injustice in this world.

We ask God why in war we were spared and the guy next to us was killed. Why them and not us? The answer: free will. God chooses not to intervene in what He has agreed to let occur. He allows people to continue with their free will and does not hit the override button. He respects us too much to take it back. As a matter of fact, it is those who choose to use their free will to be greedy, create conflict, and kill those we care about we should be angry with, not God.

God is not beholden to us. He made a decision to let us decide how things should go. Because he set into motion free will, humans often do not do the right thing – we miss the mark – and our doing so often costs other people both pain and suffering. You know what I'm talking about. You've done it; I've done it. We have, at times, caused others hurt and pain. Why? Because we are human. And why do we do some of the things we do? It goes back to those core beliefs – often because we want what we want. And kings and rulers and presidents are no different. Whatever their motives, they want what they want, and they have free will, they have weapons, and they have people at their disposal.[22]

DEALING WITH COGNITIVE DISSONANCE

A combat veteran once told me that there was no God. When I queried him, he told me there is no God because there is no heaven. To be honest, I was a little confused. I asked him to please explain in more detail, and he said, "There is no God, and there is no heaven. Because if there is a God and there is a heaven, then there is a hell, and that is where I'm going because of what I have done. Therefore, there is no God."

This particular combat veteran could not tolerate cognitive dissonance. He had to have some sort of resolution. So, he concluded there was no God because if there were, he would end up

---

[22] Nations and states also have a collective and a corporate will that they exercise, sometimes resulting in war between nations. Shakespeare wrote in *Hamlet* that nations often fight wars over ground not big enough to bury the dead. That is an ancient commentary on the senselessness of war. Yet, free will allows for that!

in hell. And the thought of hell was intolerable. So, in the end, in his mind he was left with nothing except there is no God.

I can only imagine sometimes the way God looks at us. He is probably thinking, "Hmmm. I don't exist, huh?" He knows the human heart, and he knows our pain and suffering, so much so that He was willing to send his only son to die on the cross so that we do not have to endure the consequences of our actions. Yeah, I know, I said it. I brought Jesus into this. Well, the reality is that we cannot do enough good works to earn our way into heaven. Plus, even if that were possible, there are two flaws with this logic: first, we aren't good, and we miss the mark so often that it kind of ends there. Second, when is good actually good enough? When we've done more good than bad? If that is the case, we can never have confidence that we will end up in heaven because there would have to be a measurement of goodness, and only God knows if we've done more good than bad. That leaves us with a no-confidence vote on heaven.

IS FORGIVENESS EVEN NECESSARY?

When dealing with moral injury issues and missing the mark, I have a very specific question I'd like to pose. What sin did you commit? For example, what exactly did you do that constitutes a sin? If a robber came into your home and tried to harm you or your family, would you have committed a sin if you killed him? According to God and US law, you did not. If you are authorized by the US government to be a mercenary, and you kill a terrorist, have you committed a sin? Just because a person kills someone does not mean they have sinned. I would argue that under these circumstances, one only has to look to Just War Theory to answer the question. I truly believe that there are times when combat veterans have judged themselves incorrectly, and there truly is no sin in what they have done. And some of you need to hear that right now.[23] Let me repeat that for some of you who struggle with internal voices that say the opposite. There are times when combat veterans have judged themselves incorrectly, and there truly is no sin in what they have done.

If, on the other hand, you feel as if what you did was intentional or wrong in some way and you need forgiveness, there is great news. There is one who is amazing at forgiveness. All of us have missed the mark, and as humans, we are in need of grace. It is there for the asking.[24]

GOD'S FORGIVENESS

There are multiple faith traditions that address the issue of forgiveness. I, along with most Americans, was brought up in the influence of the Judeo-Christian tradition. It is the one I can speak

---

[23] The Ten Commandments (Exodus 20:13 and Deuteronomy 5:17) discuss killing. Warriors often refer to these verses when discussing their feelings of guilt and sin. The Ten Commandments make a distinction between "murder" and a death resulting from war. God often had Israel initiate war with surrounding cultures. There are many arguments made on the subject of war, but murder and war are considered differently by God. Not recognizing this distinction has led many warriors to live with a burden of guilt that is not appropriate and is self-imposed.

[24] Many think that their personal sins are too big for God to handle, that He could never forgive them. First, that is a form of pride to think that your sin is greater than God's capacity to forgive. It is simply not true and leads to the question of what your view of God is. God is not distant or uncaring as some may imagine. He is often portrayed as a warrior, a lion, and someone to be greatly feared (see Psalms 111:10). Second, the means of forgiveness has already been accomplished through the death and resurrection of the only one who can make all things right. But a gift is useless unless taken.

to with authority. If I had grown up in other parts of the world, it is plausible that I might write from a very different faith tradition. But here we are. I will direct other religious readers to their specific faith tradition as it is beyond the scope of this book to address each and every one of them. I can only address those of you from the faith tradition in which I am trained and believe.

The America that is all-inclusive is the same as the God we serve. God makes it very clear that He is in the business of forgiveness, so if you need forgiveness, you are in luck. 1 John 1:9 says, "If you confess with your mouth, he is faithful and just and will forgive us of all sins and cleanse us from all unrighteousness." All of it. Just like in the archery example, God did not miss the mark. Not even once. He spells it out as precisely as we need to hear it. Let that sink in for a second. It's like someone offering you a free gift with one very important caveat. You have to actually accept it. You see, free gifts are not actually free. They come at a price, just like freedom. Freedom is not free. It came at the price of sacrifice and service and death. We cannot ever minimize the price that has been paid by the brothers and sisters of this great nation. The importance of this cannot be overstated.

Others have decided that our value as humans is worth the cost of their own sacrifice. They value us so much that they were, or are, willing to pay that price. And why would God and others be willing to do such a thing? Often it is because they hold an eschatological perspective.[25]

---

[25] Remember that by using this phrase, we are encouraging you to take a long-range view of life. Eschatology means the study of end times. We think that by keeping your own end in mind, you will find a more useful perspective on both your life and your purpose.

CHAPTER 10: THE RELENTLESS PURSUIT OF RESOLUTION - PERSPECTIVE AND END STATE

So how do we go about resolving issues of moral injury and survivor guilt, as well as grief and loss? In comparison to the civilian population, the military, when solving problems, often focuses on what is called the "end state," because in the military it is the outcome that matters. It is that simple. You can see it in the Army's statement: Mission First. It is the mission that must be accomplished at all cost. And what sets the parameters for the mission? The end state.

Let me use a quick example of how the end state is so important to the military mission. Let's imagine we are preparing for war. The first question Congress and the President usually ask beyond our strategic national interests is, "What is our end state?" Typically, there are two overarching goals for the end state when we go to war: to make sure that after all military operations have ceased, the country is safe and to make sure it is stable.

First, let's discuss the importance of safety. The purpose of our elected, civilian leaders to the professional military is an intent to create a safe environment, which, in essence, is the exact opposite of terrorism. In order to be safe, you have to have trust, and in this case, you have to trust that the government will protect you. Why is this so important? Because if you don't trust the governing authorities to protect you, your family, and your assets, you will do whatever you can on your own to create it.

Second, we want to create a steady, or stable, state (or nation). The reason this is important is that unstable governments set up the opportunity for power-hungry people to create havoc in people's lives. This is why people band together, many times out of either safety concerns or to gain more power, i.e., war lords/gangs. People need to feel that they are both safe and secure.

This type of end-state problem solving is very different than what most civilians are trained in. For example, most Americans start with a problem, create a hypothesis, look for solutions, and then test them. Then, depending on success or failure, they end up with an answer that may surprise them. Let me explain it this way. When going to college, most students do not know what they want to be when they "grow up." So, they take general classes in order to expand their horizons and viewpoints. As they progress through the coursework, they take elimination classes, for example, organic chemistry if they are pre-med. That class alone can impact one's future choices with regard to educational pursuits.

You can see the two different approaches to solving a problem. The military starts with the end state; whereas, civilians start at the beginning and work their way through the maze of choices toward an answer. So, the answer you get to the question, "How do I solve this problem?" will depend on whether you ask a military person who is trained in the art of end-state thinking, or a civilian trained in hypothesis testing.

USING A MILITARY MINDSET

When it comes to solving problems like PTS(D) or the invisible wounds of war, we have to choose between either hypothesis testing or an end-state perspective.

Historically, one of the challenges of dealing with military trauma is that the people who have created answers to these questions are civilian researchers trained in hypothesis testing, not end-state thinking. They begin with a disorder perspective. The assumption is that if you eliminate the person's symptoms, they will no longer meet criteria for a disorder, such as in PTS(D). They have been trained in the DSM-5, the Diagnostic and Statistical Manual of mental disorders. Again, the assumption is there is something wrong with the person.

This is in contrast to end-state thinking. Here, the focus is on what we want the person to experience, think, and feel when all is said and done.

Neither is the "right" answer, but here lies the challenge with things like moral injury and survivor guilt. The overarching answers have historically come from civilian researchers. If we continue to start with the perspective that these are disorders, we will miss alternatives or even the bigger picture.

In attempting to solve these problems, we have historically been limited to a civilian perspective. It's the difference between looking through the scope of a sniper lens versus seeing a live feed from a drone at 30,000 feet. The drone perspective can give us a lot more options to solutions because we can see a bigger field. Snipers, although very focused, are limited in their scope.

If we view the symptoms of PTS(D) through a lens or scope that calls it a "disorder," then we will most likely continue to see it from a disorder perspective. But are there ways to see these symptoms other than from a disorder perspective? Most definitely.[26]

---

[26] Different mental health providers see things differently. There are two models from which most providers practice. The medical model discovers a pathology and

So, what is an example of an alternative perspective? What the civilian world calls PTSD, the military instead calls Combat Operational Stress Reaction (COSR). This is where we are told, "What you are experiencing is a normal reaction to an abnormal situation." And what is the abnormal situation? War.

Instead of seeing trauma as a disorder, the military argues that this is a normal reaction for those who experience military trauma. Scope perspective = Disorder; Drone perspective = Normal Reaction.

The intent of research is to inform clinical practice. Research bears out that most people have a reaction to traumatic events but do not end up with a disorder. These were the findings based on research after the attacks on 9/11. Only four percent of the people who experienced 9/11 firsthand ended up with a diagnosis of PTSD a year after the twin towers fell. Four percent! That means that 96 percent did not.

The disorder viewpoint also doesn't account for people who actually experience what others have called Post-Traumatic Growth (PTG) from the experience (i.e., resilience). PTG sees the situation not through a disorder lens, but from the growth that can come out of it; again, two totally different and alternate ways of looking at trauma.

The rest of this book is dedicated to doing just that: looking at PTS(D)/COSR from an alternative viewpoint – an eschatological perspective if you will. And why again is that important? Because how you look at a problem will often influence not only your perception of the problem, but also ultimately your answer. Another influence coming from your perception or perspective is how you choose to deal with any given problem you may encounter in life. Many of the 9/11 survivors argue that they are stronger because of

_____

fixes it, while a wellness model tries to leverage the client's strength (or resiliency factors) to overcome an issue. These are just two of the models, but they see "issues" in a person's life quite differently.

what they went through. It very well may be true. "What doesn't kill you makes you stronger."

CHAPTER 11: GOD'S PERSPECTIVE - AN ESCHATOLOGICAL APPROACH

Eschatology Defined: Eschaton (ἐσχάτων) is the Greek word for end, and ology is the word for study. It is literally the study of the end. Another literal definition is *beginning with the last to the first.*[27]

VANTAGE POINT AND TIME

Because God is omniscient, He not only sees things from our perspective in time, but He can also see it from the end. God sees the whole continuum of time. And because He is God, there is no "timeframe" to which he is bound. It's kind of like watching football game film on Monday morning after you already know who won the game on Sunday. You can "watch" the film, knowing what will ultimately transpire. Even if you are down by 21 points in a football game and know the outcome, it changes the way you watch the film.

---

[27] http://biblehub.com/greek/eschato_n_2078.htm

I heard an ESPN analyst say that their job is not to state the obvious when describing a game because everyone can see what's happening. Their job is to analyze and explain how it happened or "how it came to be." They have background knowledge about the players and situations that can help the viewer understand how it is that the game unfolded the way it did. God can and does do the same thing. He is the ultimate color commentator. And it is from His vantage that the key to "perspective change" lies; an eschatological perspective, if you will.

One of our biggest challenges and downfalls as humans is that we get so focused on only seeing things from our limited perspective, we miss the big picture. We have difficulty seeing things from any other vantage point, let alone from God's perspective. All one has to do is watch how people argue. They have no problem making their points known, but to see it from the other person's perspective is a whole other challenge. I would even argue that once we reach a point where we can see things from God's perspective, the burden we carry can be lifted off our shoulders.

Allow me to use a second analogy from the perspective of a police officer.

When a police officer takes witness statements after an accident, the variances in the eyewitness accounts are quite numerous. In fact, depending on your perspective and vantage point, the police officer will most likely have as many perspectives or witness testimonies as there are witnesses. As each person begins to explain what he or she saw, each will put it in terms of time and space. Not surprising, each one of the accounts is different from the others. That is because people bring their own viewpoints, perspectives and preconceived notions to the situation. It's as if we are blinded to other options.

If you are using night vision goggles and someone turns on light, you become blinded and defenseless. There is no possibility of accomplishing your mission because you are now totally blind to your options. Our intent is to keep you from being blinded so that you can clearly see a way forward.

THE TIME-FRAME CONTINUUM – VIEWING LIFE FROM THREE DIFFERENT VANTAGE POINTS

First, what if your perspective is that tomorrow is your last day?

If you knew beyond any doubt that you were going to die tomorrow, would you be reading this book or addressing these issues? NO! You would most likely do as the psalmist said, "Eat, drink and be merry for tomorrow we shall die."[28] There is something fun, freeing and accepting about this viewpoint.

Seriously, if I knew tomorrow that I would die, I would stop writing immediately, spend time with my family, not sleep, spend whatever money I have enjoying life, and generally live it up. It's like a gambler who is all in. It's either now or never. Place your bets, and let it ride. I would make sure I invested in those things that were going to make me happy in the next 24 hours. I certainly wouldn't hold on to any assets. It's like being on the Titanic and deciding to take all of your gold with you, knowing that the weight may be the determining factor in whether your lifeboat sinks or not. If you bring it with you, you die, and there is no tomorrow.

I really want you to contemplate each of these questions and formulate an answer in your mind.

1. If you were told that you only had 24 hours to live, what would you do? Stop and think about it. What exactly would you do?

---

[28] Ecclesiastes 8:15, Isaiah 22:13, I Corinthians 15:32, and Luke 12:19

2. With whom would you spend your time?
3. What you would spend your money on?
4. Where would you go?
5. What things would go through your mind?

Anyone who is in hospice may have more than 24 hours to live, but they know their time is short. I spent eight years working as a hospice chaplain, and people who know they have a limited lifespan do not worry about tomorrow. They live as if today is their last day. They live it with no regrets. They do not care what the consequences are, they simply know that their time is fleeting, and they are not going to waste a single hour, not even a single minute, on trivial issues. There is no time for such foolishness.

I also worked with female offenders in the Federal Bureau of Prisons, and I would ask the women if they have a 401K. Many of them didn't even know what a 401K was. They have a difficult enough time trying to make it through the day financially, let alone worry about their future. And finally, anyone who has had a substance abuse problem and has been through Alcoholics Anonymous knows that you live "one day at a time," sometimes even one hour at a time.

Each of these analogies drives home the point that there is no time to waste and that consequences of actions are meaningless. People with this perspective have a foreshortened future and could care less about money or a job or anything else. As a matter of fact, when you are in a warzone and see people get killed, you, too, begin to have a foreshortened future. Why? Because people die in front of you, and you are not promised tomorrow. So, you might as well live life to the fullest. I believe this thinking is why many veterans live in adrenaline and participate in high risk behaviors.

When I was deciding which location to serve in a warzone, I had two choices: Kandahar or Kabul. I chose Kandahar because that was where most of the fighting was. Also, General Petraeus was in

Kabul, and I figured that was about as close to a green zone as one could get. I often worked in the Joint Defense Operations Center (JDOC) where all command and control were. The JDOC is one of the most secure areas inside the green zone, period. I ultimately chose Kandahar because if I were going to deploy, I might as well do whatever good I could for those on the front lines.

What I didn't know was that every one of the Air Force officers in the JDOC at Kabul during my deployment would be killed by an Afghan pilot. Yes, in the holiest of holies, the green zone, inside our most safe and secure area – the JDOC – all nine Air Force officers were killed.

As I read the news over our secure intranet, it took me a while to let the magnitude of it set in. Every one of our guys died. That means had I chosen Kabul over Kandahar, I would be dead, too. It would have been my name on the list of nine officers. Out of respect and honor, here are their names:

Lt. Col. Frank D. Bryant Jr., 37, of Knoxville, TN, who was assigned to the 56th Operations Group at Luke AFB, AZ

Maj. Philip D. Ambard, 44, of Edmonds, WA, an assistant professor of foreign languages at the US Air Force Academy in Colorado Springs, CO

Maj. Jeffrey O. Ausborn, 41, of Gadsden, AL, a C-27 instructor pilot assigned to the 99th Flying Training Squadron at Randolph AFB, TX

Maj. David L. Brodeur, 34, of Auburn, MA, an 11th Air Force executive officer at JB Elmendorf-Richardson, AK

Maj. Raymond G. Estelle II, 40, of New Haven, CT, who was assigned to Air Combat Command headquarters at JB Langley-Eustis, VA

Maj. Charles A. Ransom, 31, of Midlothian, VA, a member of the 83rd Network Operations Squadron at Langley-Eustis (posthumously promoted to the rank of major)

Capt. Nathan J. Nylander, 35, of Hockley, TX, who was assigned to the 25th Operational Weather Squadron at Davis-Monthan AFB, AZ

MSgt. Tara R. Brown, 33, of Deltona, FL, who was assigned to the Air Force Office of Special Investigations at JB Andrews, MD

Had I died, my kids would have grown up without their father. It is at times like this when one realizes how short life can be. And I believe this is one of the single most contributing factors to how combat veterans view the world, and how we view eschatology, which impacts our behavior. You see, we end up with a foreshortened future when we stare death in the face. All I can remember is wondering how many of those airmen had children that they would never see again. And those children would cry themselves to sleep knowing their fathers would never hold them in their arms.

This picture is of Christan Golczynski, age 6, after his father SSgt Marcus Golczynski was killed in Afghanistan. Permission was kindly granted by the family to use in this book.

This is the same young man ten years later. Photo by Beckimpressionsphotogrophy.com. Permission was kindly granted by the family to use in this book.

It crushes my spirit to think that my sons, Joshua and Peyton, would cry themselves to sleep at night and wonder why Daddy had to die. Unfortunately, for the families listed above, all of them have experienced that exact nightmare. My heart goes out to them in a way I cannot even begin to fathom or express.

Sometimes when things are too emotionally difficult to handle, we act. It was at that moment in Afghanistan that I took my weapon off safe. Despite any possible ROE, I wasn't going to let those around me, including the general, die without a fight. My view of my fate in this world had changed dramatically. I no longer worried about what the future held. I remembered the verse, "Do not worry about tomorrow, for tomorrow has enough worries of its own." It is at times like these that we mentally prepare for death. I also believe it is at times like this when our perspective about our place in this world changes dramatically. We realize our limited capabilities, our minuteness in this world, our value to our family, and any contributions we have made to society. In the game of chess, we realize what it really means to be a pawn. And remember, pawns are expendable. That is why there are 12 of them and only two of everything else, except, of course, a pair of royalty - the king and queen.

Many veterans believe they have a foreshortened future. They live as if they are already dead. They do not worry about tomorrow. They exhibit high risk behavior, often to continue the adrenaline rush, just to feel alive. They also do it because life is short, and they want to live it to the fullest. And this directly impacts their behavior. They fight off any anxiety or worry by saying, "Dead men don't care. And I am a dead man." They also take risks they would not have otherwise taken. Their mentality is, *when you see death squarely in the face, you shake your fist at it, and tell it to go to hell.*

I am fully convinced this foreshortened future perspective is why many veterans get themselves into trouble. They offer up threats they wouldn't otherwise make, spend money they wouldn't otherwise spend, exhibit high risk behaviors they would have never engaged in prior to war, and the list continues. There is no doubt – *war changes us.*

Even as I write this, a veteran died last week not because of suicide (which is a major problem), but because he intervened in a situation at a gas station when another man cut in line. He did what many of us in the military are trained to do. He "corrected" him! Seems civilians don't appreciate this the way we do in the military. In the end, they "took it outside" to finish their discussion, and that is when the other man pulled out a gun and shot him six times. Sometimes we create our own destiny. To say it another way, a foreshortened perspective often creates a foreshortened life.

Second, what if your perspective is seeing things from the end of your life?

If one can fight off the foreshortened future, that person may make different decisions about the future. To give an example, in the movie *Saving Private Ryan*, Captain John Miller told Private Ryan to earn the sacrifice made by his men to save Ryan. And at the end of the movie, all that Private Ryan wants to know from his wife, as he surveys the grave sites at the Normandy memorial, is if he has been a good man. That is great imagery, but more so from the moment of the death of Captain Miller, when Private Ryan lived his life with the end in mind. There is no doubt that that very fact changed the way Ryan lived his life.

Do you ask similar questions Private Ryan asked? Deep down, do you wonder if you are a good person?

This "future" may include one's normal lifespan of three score and ten, which is roughly 70 years. None of us truly know when we will die, so we plan for it in the distant future and hope we are accurate. This is the whole point of why we pay for life insurance but also plan for retirement. As a gambler, we are not all in; instead, we cover our bets in multiple ways. We pay money for term life insurance, hoping we are incorrect in that bet. We want to live a long and prosperous life, but we also hedge our bets and recognize that early death might occur, and we want our family to be well taken care of. Isn't it great that with insurance we are betting we will die, and they are betting we will live?

In this viewpoint, we take into account regrets. Why? Because most of us who have lived long enough know that we want to have as few regrets in life as possible. As compared to the example above, we do not have a "live today as if there is no tomorrow" mentality. We actually think about how our behavior affects others and ourselves. This perspective changes us from being somewhat impulsive to having a more thoughtful, end of a "good long life" perspective. We think about what we want others to say about us after we are gone. We think about what we would want listed on our headstone. It's like the guy who said, "It's the dash in between the date when you were born and when you die that matters."

The end of your life is where you not only hope you live to a "ripe old age" but your behavior also shows it. You do not "eat, drink and be merry;" instead, you think about the consequences of your actions. Instead of going to your bank account, withdrawing all the funds and spending it lavishly, you plan for the future and reject instant gratification for a future benefit. You are betting on a more promising return on your investments. You are a planner, one who looks at things with a long-term perspective. You most likely will not go all in with high-risk behaviors. You see things from an end-of-life perspective. If someone were to cut you off in traffic or in line at a gas station, you might say, "What do I care? I have the rest of my life to live. What's a few more seconds anyway?" You are more reserved, more inhibited, more future-oriented.

You can see how this perspective could alter a person's behavior. This one is from a more focused, end-of-life perspective. It takes into account one's name, what they believe in, who they are, what they want to be known for, and the impact that they may have had on others and on the world. What it is not is "instant gratification" and "impulsive." Their behavior and the decisions they make are through an end-of-life perspective and with some thought about what impact they will have made in this world.

Third, what if you have an eschatological perspective, seeing things from the perspective of "eternity"?

Let's now take a completely different viewpoint – one that surpasses human perspective and experience, one from an eschatological or "end" viewpoint. The third and final perspective is not in terms of tomorrow, or even the end of life, but eternity, or more specifically, the beginning of eternity starting with the day you stand before God: Judgment Day.

When I ask combat veterans to write down their end state, it is their perspective on *when* they will die that surfaces. Think about how your behavior is heavily influenced by answering just this one question: if you believed that tomorrow you would die, how would you live today?

Or if you believe you will live to a normal age, how will that change your behavior and even your financial strategy about living?

Finally, if you live your life from an eschatological (eternal) perspective, how will that influence your life and what you do?

Now is when the critics begin to come out. Some inevitably will ask, "But what about a person who doesn't believe in God or eternity?" Well, then they have to make decisions in their life based on what they do believe. Some believe in Karma, some believe in Buddha, others in native American ideology, some in annihilation theory. Whatever one's beliefs, I highly recommend you look at the correlation between what one believes and how one acts.

Let's take for a moment the perspective of a belief in God and a belief in eternity – a true eschatological perspective. If you believe that you will be judged for eternity on how you behaved and what you did with your life here on earth, would that change how you live? If you thought for one second that God was keeping track of everything you did, good or bad, would that change your behavior? Even more so, God says that the things done in secret will be revealed. Would that change things?

People act very differently when they think others will not find out about what they have done. The eternity perspective I'm proposing says that even that which is done in secret will be revealed. What if this life is a precursor to eternity? All of a sudden, when one considers that this may very well be a reality, you no longer have to wonder if people "will get theirs." They will. In fact,

God not only knows what people do out in the open and in secret, but He also knows their heart. So much for others "getting away with it." When you are wronged, God even goes so far as to say, "Revenge is mine sayeth the Lord, I will repay." And think about that for a second if you have been wronged. Do you think for one second that you can decipher what is not only in someone's heart but also the judgment they deserve? You cannot, but God can.

God not only knows the heart, but He also has an arsenal of weapons when it comes to judgment. One does not have to worry about "getting even" or that judgment will fall on their head. Instead, *God will* repay. I would *not* want to be in their shoes. But then again, I don't even want to be in mine when it comes to God's judgement. I would much rather beg for forgiveness than suffer God's wrath. You see, this is exactly why people want mercy when they are the ones who have done wrong. But when one has been wronged, we demand justice. Our response depends on whether we are the ones wronged or the ones who have done wrong.

What this does then is bring into perspective God's ability to judge people. It is no longer our responsibility to judge; we can leave it up to God. *And when we do this, it completely takes away the need for revenge.* If we truly believe it, and God does act on our behalf, what do you think it would do to our anger? I argue that it dissipates. As a matter of fact, the more we understand the magnitude of God's wrath, the more we may not even want it for our enemies. But then, we might.

An eschatological perspective also changes the way we view death. In an eschatological perspective, death is just the beginning of eternity. Your buddy who got killed – he's in eternity. And us? We are in the process of getting there. You see, when our perspective changes, everything changes, especially when we begin to see this life from God's perspective. When you can see things from His eyes, from His vantage point, from His characteristics, it changes everything. There is no need to demand justice, because God will be the one who does exactly that.

- If you wonder if others will ever get their punishment for what they did, the answer is yes.
- If you wonder if you will ever be rewarded for the things you did out of pure motives, the answer is yes.
- If you wonder if there is justice in the world, the answer is yes.
- If you wonder if the person who did horrible, egregious acts will ever be discovered and brought to justice, the answer is yes.
- If you wonder if God is able to see the human heart and judge accordingly, the answer is yes.
- If you wonder if God will ever stop the pain and suffering and bring about His characteristics of love, kindness, justice, and mercy, the answer is a resounding YES!
- If you wonder if this is all for naught, the answer is no. Everything we do matters. Everything.

God gave us free will, and what we do with it matters. And thank God (pun intended) because we need it. *We need a God who will ultimately make it right.* It's like our parents to whom we turn when we are tired and weary and just need rest. We can fall into their arms and fall asleep knowing that all is okay in this world. We know that our parents love us unconditionally and will do anything for us.[29] God's love is the same. He even tells us, "Come to me all

---

[29] It should be understood here that one of the main risk factors for PTS(D) is a dysfunctional relationship with parents prior to military service. Thus, many suffering with PTS(D) have never known a loving, fulfilling relationship with their parents. This makes visualizing God as the perfect parent difficult for many. Those who have been damaged by their relationship to their parents will have to consider

you who are weary and heavy laden, and I will give you rest."[30] His characteristics prevail. He is both loving and just. He will bring about justice and mercy. He is, after all, God.

So, in the end, all is not in vain. Our buddies who died did not die in vain. They will receive their reward in heaven[31] for their sacrifices, and God will divvy out rewards in a just and right manner based on what we have done here on earth. God will make it right. In that, we can have confidence. Our buddies who died, their time was up. But we, we have time on our side. **The only question is, what will we do with the time we have left?**

We are accountable for what we do with it. We get to choose. We can remain vengeful, angry, defiant and demand justice for the wrongdoing, but it is not time. That time will come. We only have so much time left before we, too, stand before God, and it is far better to use our time productively than it is to demand that which God is already going to do – bring about justice and, sometimes, wrath. Can you even imagine the intensity of God's wrath for one second? It will be interesting to watch when the time comes, but you don't want to be on the wrong side of His justice when it does. Not just justice, but the implementation of that justice. God will unleash his wrath on certain individuals because they have used their free will and caused so much pain and heartache. Remember, "Revenge is mine sayeth, the Lord, I will repay."[32]

Instead, this is our time. God has given us, even *us*, free will. And what will you do with the time you have remaining? It is, after all, limited. For not only have we all fallen short of perfection, all

---

this more extensively to understand God's love for them, but surely it will help them understand what is possible and that will ultimately prove valuable to them.

[30] Matthew 11:28

[31] Assuming that their name is written in the Lamb's Book of Life

[32] Romans 12:9 and Deuteronomy 32:35

before us have or will die. We all end up before God at some point. The question is what will you do with the time you have left?

As you may have noticed, I tried to do in this book what I believe we should do in life. I started with the "answer." The answer to many of life's questions, even difficult questions such as "Why did my buddy have to die?" starts with an eschatological perspective. Instead of seeing it only from our vantage point in time, we thrust ourselves into answers of an eternal nature that can only be answered in the context of eternity. The answer is found in truly appreciating and accepting an eschatological viewpoint. When we have this, and have confidence in the fact that God is God and His perfect justice and mercy will prevail, we do not have to wonder how or why the situation came about. It happened because men and women have free will. Others made choices that put us and them in a certain place in time. And because it is a battle of the will, we were often the pawn on the chessboard. Unfortunately, our buddy next to us is also a pawn. And pawns are expendable (at least to some).

What we need is the perspective from the Grand Master, the one who not only sees the game that is being played, but also has the power and authority to change the game. God is, after all, the ultimate game changer.

In this process, I have argued for an eschatological response to difficult questions. And why not? It is, after all, *the* answer. Sometimes, we need answers up front. We need to know that all is truly going to work out in the end. Sometimes it's good to already know who won the game before you watch it on the DVR. And how can we be certain in knowing this is how it is going to play out? Because God is God. His characteristics do not change. And they certainly don't change based on what we believe. They are immutable. They do not shift. They do not falter; they are forever embedded for eternity as long as God is God. Simply put, we can bank on it.

Now that we have our end-state perspective, let's work our way back in time to where people are. Because meeting people where they are, not where we wish they were, is the key.

Our intent in this book is to answer the specific questions of moral injury and survivor guilt. But we will do so from an eschatological viewpoint - in reverse order when it comes to time, if you will.

APPLYING AN ESCHATOLOGICAL PERSPECTIVE

Now that I have described the three perspectives from which we choose to "see" our place in this world, let's look at how this affects our thought patterns, our emotions, and ultimately, our behavior. You may not have consciously given this much thought, but there is a direct, positive correlation between one's view of death and one's accountability for one's actions. If you truly believe you will die tomorrow, you will act accordingly. If, on the other hand, you believe in an eschatological perspective, you will most likely act very differently. Remember, eschatology is seeing things from the end (i.e., the big picture).

So, how does this affect what we want out of life and our "end state"?

As we think about those things that are the most important to us, we need to consciously make decisions about our investment in them. When asking combat veterans to list out their end state, they inevitably create a list of things to include: family, faith, friends, finances, etc. As a matter of fact, if you haven't created the things that you value the most, now is the time. Let's once and for all create our end state of what is important.

Please take the time to seriously contemplate the questions and then complete the blanks. We will use this information in the coming chapter.

1. When it comes to family, I value:

_____

_____

2. When it comes to faith, I value:

_____

_____

3. When it comes to finances, I value:

_____

_____

4. When it comes to _____, I value:

_____

_____

5. When it comes to _____, I value:

_____

_____

6. When it comes to _____, I value:

_____

_____

CHAPTER 12: PRACTICAL APPLICATION OF END STATE AND ESCHATOLOGY

N ow that you've created your list, let's talk about how this can affect your future and your behavior. Take, for example, the first one – family. Who did you list as important to you? Is there anyone in whom you want to invest your life? Maybe it's your spouse. Or maybe someone left you, and there is a void, and this brings up difficult emotions. Even so, there is probably someone you care about. List that person.

Let's say for the sake of brevity that you listed your spouse or significant other. You decide that what you value about your end state includes them. Now, how important is that person to you? Very? Okay, if you didn't write their name down, please do so now.

Now, let's take a specific scenario. Let's say that it just happens to be your spouse's birthday, and you want to treat her or him to something special. You are both dressed up and on the freeway, heading to the restaurant of their choosing. On your way to the restaurant, someone who is driving erratically swerves and cuts you off in traffic. Your initial response is very focused, and anger begins to set in. You may even revert back in time to when you were in a convoy and how you were taught to mitigate risk at all cost. No matter what, you remind yourself, you do not stop. And because we believe in correcting people in the military and have been taught this repeatedly, you want to teach this guy a lesson.

Remember, we are taught in the military to mitigate risk. This guy is a risk, so you take it upon yourself to do something. It should be no surprise that military members are one of the first people to act. If you remember the commercial for the Marines on the battlefield, there is chaos everywhere, and a guy is calling you forward. And the caption asks, "Which way will you run?" Well, military members, police, firefighters, EMTs, etc., all run toward danger, not away from it.

So, you speed up, and before you know it, you are doing 90 mph. All the while, your spouse is telling you to slow down. We are not bystanders; we are initiators by nature. Your driving is intentional, and you want with everything inside you to stop this guy from driving the way he is. God only knows that he can get someone killed. In pursuing him, you begin to lose your eschatological perspective and go into instant gratification. In essence, you are going to do what you want. And you want this guy to stop, and you believe it's your job to do it. In this process, you lose perspective on your spouse's concern about safety and security. Your spouse wants you to stop because it makes her or him anxious, fearful. And God only knows what kind of crazy lunatic is behind the wheel of the other car.

It is at that moment that your two beliefs collide - your belief in teaching this guy a lesson and mitigating the risk he can cause versus your belief that your spouse is more important than anyone else.

What would you do? Do you teach this guy a lesson, or do you put your spouse's needs first? If you think of it in terms of investment, in whom do you want to invest? Your spouse whom you listed as a priority in your end state, or someone you most likely do not even know? By going after this erratic driver, you are basically telling your spouse that you do not care about him or her, that your spouse's needs are less important than your need to teach this guy a lesson. You are then challenged to make a decision. To whom will you give your care, concern, and energy? To a stranger, or to your spouse? It is at times like these that we have to stop and think about in whom and what we want to invest. Could you teach this guy a lesson? Of course, but at what price? Simple – at the price of your relationship with your spouse.

Some of you completely understand the point I have just made. Others may not, but hopefully, you will see how it is that what we choose to invest in ultimately affects what we do.

WHICH VOICE WILL YOU LISTEN TO?

We've talked about the issue of how people may have cognitive dissonance about why they are still here on this earth, which may or may not be resolved to their liking. Ultimately, it would be great if God were to just speak into our ear when we ask, "Why did I survive when my buddy died?" In the quietness of those moments, when all is silent, we can hear very loud voices – mantras,[33] if you will - about what we have concluded and what we tell ourselves. And what we conclude did not happen overnight. It is a culmination of experiences and thoughts and beliefs that bring us to this point. And without God speaking directly to us, we are left constantly thinking and rethinking and evaluating and reevaluating.

Unfortunately, sometimes the thoughts we come to accept are unhealthy and can be unrelenting. It is, after all, these thoughts and mantras about who we are that keep us up at night.

---

[33] Another phrase for "mantras" as used here is "self-talk."

Have you gotten to the point that you just point blank ask God "why?"

- Why did this have to happen?
- Why did they have to die?
- Why did I survive?

But God remains silent. If only He would answer us.

I believe God will ultimately answer these questions. But it is also very possible that He may not answer in this lifetime. So, where does that leave us? With some basic facts.

1. You are still here. That cannot be debated. I intentionally did not say "alive" because many do not feel it.
2. What you do with the time you have left matters. It matters not only to you, but to those around you. It also matters to God.
3. Without a mission and a purpose, we are aimless. It's like a sniper without a target. No need to explain. We need both!

So now what?

With regard to survivor guilt and moral injury, I would like to propose a weightlifting exercise. No, not PT, thank God. In essence, I'd like the weight of this burden taken from you by the time you finish this chapter. A tall order? Perhaps, but an endeavor worthy of the energy it requires.

The challenge with survivor guilt and moral injury is that even if those affected deal with the shame and guilt itself, they often feel as if they cannot let go of it, lest the memory of their fallen comrades be lost in vain. I believe this is exactly the opposite of what will happen. Instead of losing those memories, one regains one's life and honors fallen comrades by living a life worth living. Let me explain.

Let's be clear. The only way to really know why you are still here is to have God himself tell you. And the last I checked, neither you nor I have the capability to make that happen. Oh, but if only we did. Life is often about ambiguity and uncertainty. Some have even suggested that the key to life is accepting that things are constantly changing and that nothing stays the same. The sooner we accept this, the easier it is to accept life in general.[34]

But no matter what your view is on change, I do find comfort in knowing that God can change the outcome of any hand we have been dealt. And although others may not have set the stage for what you are going through, remember, "What man meant for evil, God can use for good."[35] God has the ability to take any situation, no matter how bleak, and turn it 180 degrees. Allow me the honor and privilege of sharing a personal experience of God at work. My hope is that you can relate to this example, even if the circumstances are different.

GETTING MARRIED AND CHOOSING TO SEE THINGS FROM GOD'S PERSPECTIVE

My fiancée and I had both come out of difficult relationships, and, to be honest, we had felt the sting and pain of divorce. Feeling

---

[34] To truly understand the eschatological perspective requires an even larger perspective, which is to have an understanding of God himself. Perfect understanding is not possible, but enough so that these matters become clearer. It has often been said that if you want to understand yourself, you must understand God. This is true in that if you see the world from a larger perspective (His), your relationship to our finite, smaller world becomes clearer.

[35] Genesis 50:20–21

broken, the last thing we wanted to do was re-experience that hurt and pain. But there we were, writing our vows to each other the day before we were to get married and me trying to put words together that would illustrate what I saw God capable of doing in our marriage. I needed something to change in my life. I needed to not see this marriage from my perspective as I had done previously. I had already caused enough pain and suffering and experienced it as well. I needed to shift my focus. I needed to see this marriage from God's perspective. I needed an eschatological perspective, not only because I hoped for a better outcome, but also to change me at the core to do what I needed to do to make it work.

I needed God himself to help me see what a healthy, happy marriage could look like. But I also needed to deal with my past and to somehow find a way to make it all fit. What God wanted from me was to see this marriage from His viewpoint, not mine. So, I set my mind on seeing things from God's perspective, as scary as it might be. You see, giving up control is not in my nature. I like to be in charge, but clearly, my way was not always the right way. I wonder if you can relate?

As I began to write my vows, I decided to use the analogy of broken glass. My previous marriage was very unhealthy, mostly because I was selfish. I regrettably believe that I was the cause of most of our troubles and unhappiness. Of course, it takes two, but I truly believe in my heart that it was my fault. I take full responsibility. And where did that leave me? There were times in my life that I felt my life was completely shattered.

It was as if one moment I was looking into a mirror at who I truly was, and the next moment my fist was in pain, my fingers bloody, and the mirror was broken into a hundred pieces. At the time, I sometimes wondered how my life had gotten to that point. I didn't ask for some of the things I had gone through to happen, and not only did I not like what I saw in the mirror, but I was also the one who had shattered it. Maybe you feel the same way at times. You look down and see brokenness all around you. There are shattered pieces of your life just lying there. Some things happen to us, and some things we cause. You can see some large pieces, some small, but all very sharp. Danger awaits anyone who dares touch them. You may even feel as if you have very little defense against the pain of even attempting to put things back together. And you somehow know that no matter how well you put it back together again, it will never be as good as it was originally. Life has dealt you a very sharp hand - a very sharp hand indeed!

One can feel very much alone at moments like this. Standing there, staring at a broken life and broken glass, wondering, "is this all there is? Is there more to life than just this? Is there any chance to even fix what has been broken?"[36]

But knowing the risk, you take it. You slowly attempt to put the pieces of your life back together, being ever so gentle, knowing that the sharp edges cut like a serrated knife. And God knows you've already bled enough. You know the pain that this world can bring. Whether it happens *to* us, or *we* are the cause of it, the effect is still very much the same – a life broken,[37] shattered and in pieces.

---

[36] At a very critical point in my life, I [(MH)] participated in a joint military SERE course in Germany. On a day during which I became hypothermic due to exposure to horrendous weather conditions, I became exhausted from moving up and down the mountains in the German Black Forest region, so much so that I literally sat down in a mud puddle. But as clear as day, I thought to myself that if my life was any indication of the struggle to come, then I seriously doubted whether my life was worth living. The only exception to that thought was a feeling that if there is a God, then there could be an explanation to the perceived misery. I left that muddy mountainside that day convinced that the only goal worth pursuing was finding God; otherwise, life had no meaning and seemed futile. I had found a purpose, perhaps even a passion, that superseded the misery I felt at that moment.

[37] And no broken person suffers on an island . . . there is always collateral damage in a broken life!

In survivor guilt and moral injury, I often felt as if a good friend of mine hit the nail on the head. Ms. Sarah Kemp is her name, and she is a writer. She also works for the USO. After one of our friends was killed in Kandahar, Afghanistan, she wrote the title to a blog about Darren Hidalgo, an Army First Lieutenant who graduated from West Point. It was entitled, "The Sharp Knife of a Short Life." It's the same idea of feeling the sharp pain from a life that was taken way too early. It is irreversible and heartbreaking. It is the life breath or spirit that has been snuffed out. It is from the Hebrew word (רוח), pronounced Ruach. I picture a birthday candle that has been blown out, only instead of there being 90 candles on the cake, it only has 19 – too few candles for someone who is supposed to live a full life.

Whatever the analogy, whether it is the sharp edge of a knife or shards of glass, it illustrates the brokenness and pain we often experience from death. Life beckons us to move forward, but sometimes it's hard to even move.

TIME FOR A NEW PERSPECTIVE

After I experienced a spinal cord injury/illness in Kandahar, I was sent to Landstuhl Regional Medical Center (LRMC). LRMC is by far one of the best hospitals in the world. Not only do they ensure that our service men and women are well taken care of, but they also take personal pride in doing so. One of the best solutions they have for those of us coming out of the Area of Responsibility (AOR) is the integration of the chaplains into their holistic approach. Their investment in my life was indispensable.

I love chaplains. They are amazing people who truly have a heart for doing good. While at LRMC, between the MRIs, blood work, physical therapy, and every possible test known to man, I had the option to sign up through the chaplain's ministry for a sightseeing tour. They take you out into the beautiful countryside of Germany and help you begin the transition back home, mentally. On my trip, we went to a city I do not recall, but what I do remember is seeing the largest church I have ever seen in my life. The church was bigger than a football field and was taller than an eight-story building. It was massive. But what was even more massive was the beauty of the stained glass.

The stained glass allowed just enough light in to see every color God created, every color in the rainbow you can imagine, radiating in a way that brought out the beauty of God's creation in pictures. Words simply cannot describe the artistic beauty that had been created. It felt as if hope had grabbed me and was holding me tight with no intention of letting me go. And what was the purpose of the stained glass?

Those stained-glass windows were the stories of the faith of the men and women from the Bible on full display, in all their grandeur. Some of the pictures had to have been at least 30 feet tall, one picture story after another of God's redeeming grace. And of course, it was in no other place than in Germany, a country we had destroyed with our bombing raids during WWII. As a matter of fact, I am certain that this church was intentionally spared by the US and our allies during the bombings. The churches may have felt the reverberation of bombs exploding around them, but many of them were spared. Very seldom did I ever see dilapidated buildings in Germany because most of them were destroyed in WWII. It's a beautiful country with rolling hills, the Rhine river, and miles and miles of green grass. It's something of a beauty I had never experienced. Even Disney's Magic Kingdom highlights the real castle that is in Germany.

And what does this all have to do with our broken and shattered lives? Remember the broken pieces of your life that are strewn around your feet? They remind you of the hand you have been dealt. They remind you that things were not supposed to turn out this way. And there are the broken and shattered pieces that have your dead buddy's blood on them. Every one of those pieces reminds you of how painful life can be. And so, we have to make a decision, a decision to see things from our own perspective, or from God's perspective, and the possibilities that exist. God is still in the business of doing amazing things in people's lives. Even yours. But it requires something from you. It requires you to see what you are going through from God's perspective.[38]

Those stained-glass windows throughout this massive church highlighted and showcased God himself in a way I had never experienced. A country ravaged by war from Hitler and his entourage was now a sanctuary for people like me who had been serving in Afghanistan and other places, a refuge in times of trouble and a reminder that God can turn brokenness into beauty.

It requires someone, an artist, who can see things from God's perspective. Anyone can see shattered glass, but can you see God's story about your life written and displayed in all its splendor? It's like when Michelangelo chiseled David out of stone. David was in there, he just needed to get rid of everything that got in the way of our seeing him. So, what is it that needs to be chiseled away from you? What is it that continues to "hang on" and burden you? What needs a hammer taken to it so that God's masterpiece that is your life can be revealed?

---

[38] J. Sidlow Baxter (1903-1999) was an English pastor, who in a conference in Germany once said, "God is more interested in changing your character than your circumstances." It is a change in perspective that requires you to make a choice about what, or perhaps who, you will believe.

It doesn't take *vision* to see broken lives and shattered glass. It doesn't take *vision* to see beyond despair. What seeing from God's perspective requires is that we see things from a totally different vantage point. We have to see it from a different place in time, from a different perspective, for a different purpose. And this is exactly what the artists of the stained glass were able to do. The question is, do you have what it takes to get rid of that which so easily hinders you and instead be the artist of your life?

The shattered glass is our brokenness, our lives on full display for others to see. You can continue living your life as if you are broken like some are doing. You can even put it on full display with hats and shirts that say, "Stay back, I have PTS(D)." You can let PTS(D) become your identity, or you can choose to see things from God's perspective.

The shattered glass of your life could be left as rubble to be walked on, destroyed, or ground up and recycled. ***But no, not you, and not this glass.*** This is the same rubble, the same broken pieces that are to be shaped. And how do we do that? The same way the artist who created the Sistine chapel did it. You have to see your circumstances and the hand you have been dealt from God's perspective. The question is, do you have what it takes to see things from God's perspective?

We are God's artists. We, too, can be inspired to create beauty. The same artist who sculpted and created these beautiful works of art is the same human artist who was inspired by God to see the world from His perspective. And what did it require? Five Ts: Time, Tools, Talent, Tenacity, and a Totally different perspective.

God's artists methodically placed the broken pieces of stained glass and laid them out in such an array that they brought God's perspective to light. Literally. It required a person to shift from seeing human reality to seeing reality from God's perspective. You see, if all you do is see it from where you are standing, it's just broken glass strewn around you. But to see it from God's perspective, it becomes an opportunity to show His creativity and ability to turn brokenness into beauty. And it's not just about the hand we are dealt, it's also about how we approach life and see things through His eyes. We are not alone in this. Others have faced very similar circumstances. There are countless men and women in the Bible who made the decision to see life from God's perspective. They don't just see their reality; they create their reality. They intentionally forego what they see in front of them and choose instead to see it from and through God's eyes. And this totally changes not only our perspective – it changes how we live our lives!

DANIEL AND THE LION'S DEN

Remember good old Daniel and the Lion's Den? You know the one where he was purportedly destined to become lion food? The king had made a decree that **anyone who prayed to any other God would be put to death**. It was simple and straight forward. And there were those who used this to their advantage and had evil intent. Starting to sound familiar? You, trying to do the right thing when others are intent on death and destruction? You, trying to bring about safety and security while others are hell bent on creating chaos? Well, Daniel also experienced this. Most people know the story, but in this instance, I don't want you to see the obvious. I want you to open your aperture. Look beyond seeing Daniel and his faith. Look beyond how God spared his life; although, when lions are at your door, being rescued at this point in your life might sound really appealing. Let's not miss what actually happened to... *the king.*

King Darius created a decree that could not be changed. He had written it in such a way that there were *no exceptions, no options, no way out!* Although King Darius deeply respected Daniel, it was either break his own law or make Daniel face the consequences. In a strange way, King Darius actually kept his integrity. He did what he said he would do. Although it would cost him dearly, he felt he had no other choice. Maybe you've been in those situations as well. Choices have been made, situations presented, and consequences happened.

As you know, the king chose to have Daniel thrown into the lion's den rather than retract his decree and lose his integrity. Integrity comes at a price, and sometimes others pay it. Sometimes in life, people make bad decisions and feel they no longer have a choice. They are stuck and see no way out. The king made an edict, Daniel broke it, and so Daniel had to face the lions.

King Darius was the one who created the situation. He was the one who demanded death for dereliction. The death of Daniel was going to be on his hands. So, what did the king do? Did he put a stop to the situation? No, he did not. Did he void the edict? Nope. Did he demand mercy? No.

This king was different. This king had witnessed Daniel in action. He knew Daniel to be a man of faith, and this was going to be the real test of his faith, so much so that it was actually the king himself who saw this situation from God's perspective. Yes, it was actually the king who believed that God could save Daniel.

The king actually did two things.

First, he followed through on his promise. He did not break his edict. But even more important is what the king did next.

The king chose to see the situation from God's perspective. Let's read it.

Daniel in the Den of Lions [39]

1. It pleased Darius to appoint 120 satraps to rule throughout the kingdom, *2.* with three administrators over them, one of whom was Daniel. The satraps were made accountable to them so that the king might not suffer loss. *3.* Now Daniel so distinguished himself among the administrators and the satraps by his exceptional qualities that the king planned to set him over the whole kingdom. *4.* At this, the administrators and the satraps tried to find grounds for charges against Daniel in his conduct of government affairs, but they were unable to do so. They could find no corruption in him, because he was trustworthy and neither corrupt nor negligent. *5.* Finally, these men said, "We will never find any basis for charges against this man Daniel unless it has something to do with the law of his God."

6. So these administrators and satraps went as a group to the king and said: "May King Darius live forever! *7.* The royal administrators, prefects, satraps, advisers and governors have all agreed that the king should issue an edict and enforce the decree that anyone who prays to any god or human being during the next thirty days, except to you, Your Majesty, shall be thrown into the lions' den. *8.* Now, Your Majesty, issue the decree and put it in writing so that it cannot be altered—in accordance with the law of the Medes and Persians, which cannot be repealed." *9.* So King Darius put the decree in writing.

10. Now when Daniel learned that the decree had been published, he went home to his upstairs room where the windows opened toward Jerusalem. Three times a day he got down on his knees and prayed, giving thanks to his God, just as he had done before. *11.* Then these men went as a group and found Daniel praying and asking God for help. *12.* So they went

---

[39] Daniel 6, quoted from the New International Version (NIV) Bible

to the king and spoke to him about his royal decree: "Did you not publish a decree that during the next thirty days anyone who prays to any god or human being except to you, Your Majesty, would be thrown into the lions' den?"

The king answered, "The decree stands—in accordance with the law of the Medes and Persians, which cannot be repealed."

13. Then they said to the king, "Daniel, who is one of the exiles from Judah, pays no attention to you, Your Majesty, or to the decree you put in writing. He still prays three times a day." *14.* When the king heard this, he was greatly distressed; he was determined to rescue Daniel and made every effort until sundown to save him.

15. Then the men went as a group to King Darius and said to him, "Remember, Your Majesty, that according to the law of the Medes and Persians no decree or edict that the king issues can be changed."

16. So the king gave the order, and they brought Daniel and threw him into the lions' den. The king said to Daniel, "May your God, whom you serve continually, rescue you!"

17. A stone was brought and placed over the mouth of the den, and the king sealed it with his own signet ring and with the rings of his nobles, so that Daniel's situation might not be changed. *18.* Then the king returned to his palace and spent the night without eating and without any entertainment being brought to him. And he could not sleep.

19. At the first light of dawn, the king got up and hurried to the lions' den. *20.* When he came near the den, he called to Daniel in an anguished voice, "Daniel, servant of the living God, has your God, whom you serve continually, been able to rescue you from the lions?"

21. Daniel answered, "May the king live forever! *22.* My God sent his angel, and he shut the mouths of the lions. They have not hurt me, because I was found innocent in his sight. Nor have I ever done any wrong before you, Your Majesty."

23. The king was overjoyed and gave orders to lift Daniel out of the den. And when Daniel was lifted from the den, no wound was found on him, because he had trusted in his God.

24. At the king's command, the men who had falsely accused Daniel were brought in and thrown into the lions' den, along with their wives and children. And before they reached the floor of the den, the lions overpowered them and crushed all their bones.

25. Then King Darius wrote to all the nations and peoples of every language in all the earth:

"May you prosper greatly!

26. "I issue a decree that in every part of my kingdom people must fear and reverence the God of Daniel.

*"For he is the living God
and he endures forever;
his kingdom will not be destroyed,
his dominion will never end.*

*27. He rescues and he saves;
he performs signs and wonders
in the heavens and on the earth.
He has rescued Daniel
from the power of the lions."*

28. So Daniel prospered during the reign of Darius and the reign of Cyrus^a the Persian.

The point is that the king had the ability to see this situation that even he had created from God's perspective. He had seen in Daniel's faith that his God could save him. And although there is still a question in his voice about whether or not he knew what would happen, it was this perspective that helped him to fast and pray and wait expectantly in the morning. Then the king ran to the lions' den because he had hope and a belief that God would save

Daniel, that there would be an outcome different than the one he, as king, had decreed.

You see, whether God saves us or not, the point is clear. If we can see things from God's perspective, everything changes. It is this perspective that gives us hope and a future. Instead of simply seeing the tragedy of a death sentence before us, we have the free will and ability to experience something far greater. We can actually act and move in a particular direction with faith that God himself can and may do something amazing. We may not know the outcome until much later. Maybe not even in this lifetime. But if we can tear away everything that gets in the way, similar to what Michelangelo did in the sculpting of David, we can then see the hand of God. In this beautiful sculpture, it is not only the beauty of David that is amazing as much as it is the artist's ability to see David from God's perspective. Michelangelo literally could see what David would look like inside a piece of granite. It was his job to get rid of everything else that kept us from seeing David in that statue.

And what gets in the way of our seeing our true inner self and the beauty that God has created? The voices inside and outside our head that tell us there is no hope. The voices that keep us staring at the brokenness scattered around our feet. The mantras that we repeat to ourselves: that it is our fault, that we are to blame, that we did this, or we didn't do that. No! We must get out of our limited vision and see things from God's perspective.

Sometimes people wonder why God took a life. It just doesn't make sense why he would "need another angel in heaven" or whatever so called "answers" people come up with. The reality is that God didn't. God doesn't need anything. Instead, it is highly plausible in this viewpoint that free will was involved and that is what cost your friend his life.

We, too, have a choice. We can continue seeing things from our perspective, which is often debilitating, or we can choose to see things from God's perspective. It is a radical shift, but one that brings true hope and healing.

Daniel was spared. The king could envision God at work. It was right in front of him, but he actually had to believe and see it from God's perspective. What will you do? Will you trust God and move beyond your brokenness and what you "see" in front of you? Or will you make a willful decision to move past the hand the world has dealt you and let God be in charge of the next phase of your life? It takes work, and help.[40] Mental, physical, and spiritual work. But one thing is certain, we have seen God do amazing things over and over again. So why not you, and why not now? Why not let God write His story of your life for all to see? Your life will, after all, be a testimony no matter what. The question is, what will it say? What do you want your legacy to be?

God takes the broken of this world and creates beauty. He puts his vision into the mind of men and women and helps them to see it from His perspective. He gave the vision to those who could create beautiful works of art in the Sistine chapel from glass and create it in such a way that you can see, feel, and visualize His hand at work in the midst of chaos and in the face of death. He is a God that does not sit back and do nothing. Do not confuse patience with idleness. He is patient, and He is taking note. Not for his benefit, but for ours. You see, what we make of the brokenness is up to us. Sure, a sharp knife or broken glass can be used to cut people deeply in a way that destroys them, but in the hands of a surgeon it can be a scalpel to heal.

---

[40] Because we humans have such limited perspective, we often need help to see things differently. As psychologists and counselors, we major in helping people see things from a different, more helpful perspective. But there are others in your life who may be just as helpful (such as pastors, or supportive, wise friends) if you are open to receive their input.

The broken pieces of our lives can be arranged in such a way as to put them alongside resin, not only to keep them in place, but also to fill in the cutting edges that can cause more damage. Instead, they are encased so that it is as smooth as glass, literally. Beautiful stained glass, picturesque beyond measure. Light that shines through where darkness cannot hide. Remember the church with the stained glass? As I stood there, I realized that brokenness is not the only answer. The sharp knife of a short life does not have to be the end. We can turn tragedy into God's story of our lives. It does not have to be in vain, and it does not have to define or destroy us.

The demons that haunt our inner being have no choice but to be driven out and flee when we choose to take what has crushed us and use it in a way that brings people and ourselves into a healing place, a sanctuary; a place of rest and peace and serenity. The choice is ours. It is yours today.

Cautiously, patiently, and methodically with God's perspective in mind, we can place the broken pieces of our lives in an array that will ultimately bring forth light, light that shines through with the various colors of the rainbow in green and blue and red and yellow and purple. Vibrant colors that were once shattered pieces of glass can show forth God's light from the sun. It is, once again, our choice to do with it what we will. It was a choice that caused harm, death, and evil. It is a choice that creates serenity, peace, and life. So, whatever you take from this book, take this to heart. What you choose to do with the brokenness of this life and the sharp, cutting edge of a knife or broken glass is up to you. God has given you the freedom to choose. What you make of brokenness and what we sometimes perceive as a life that was needlessly taken from us is up to you. It is their memory, their life, their sacrifice that can live on in what we do.

SO, WHERE EXACTLY IS GOD IN ALL THIS?

God is exactly where he has been all along. Being God. The way I see it, God has, at minimum, three options:

1. God intervenes. Sometimes He chooses to intervene, and we see His direct impact. Sometimes He chooses to intervene, and we don't even know it.

2. God does not intervene. Just as we have free will, so does God. God is consistent in that His free will is consistent with his character. We may not know at this moment why He did not intervene, but God is omniscient, omnipotent and omnipresent. Nothing gets by Him. God also loves us. Therefore, for whatever reason, the decision is based on the big picture. If you looked at it from Job's perspective, Job may have really wondered whether God was going to intervene or not. It certainly wasn't because God wasn't willing or interested; God had a bigger point to make. And he allowed – yes, allowed – Job to be the conduit. During trials and tribulations, no one enjoys being the conduit. However, when all is said and done, I would bet that Job would have it no other way. To know that God himself believed in Job so much that he set him up as a pawn to be afflicted by Satan himself. God had only one rule: you can't kill him, but the rest was fair game. Job was tried and tested and yet refused to curse God and die. 2,000 years later, and we still know of this man called Job. Job clearly had an eschatological perspective!

3. God chooses to be patient. Waiting patiently and taking notes. Watching, observing, waiting. He may intervene way

128

after we thought He should have intervened, but nonetheless, God has his reasoning. It is clear in scripture that the reason why God continues to be patient with all of humanity is that he is wanting none to perish. Talk about a loving God! A God who is so patient, He continues to allow evil and free will to wreak havoc in this world so that none will perish. God clearly has an eschatological mindset. But alas, even His patience will one day end. I imagine when that happens, He will say "**Enough**!" in a voice loud enough that people will hear it throughout the world at the same time. His commanding voice with one word will change all of humanity. Enough pain and suffering, enough evil, enough of this chaos. Enough is enough! In the twinkling of an eye, it will end. And end abruptly. And judgment will come.

But until that day, He is patient, very patient with us and our humaneness. And why again does He do this? So that all can come to know Him. He takes it. He takes the questions, and He hears the cries. He hears the threats and the questions and the pain, and He knows. He knows firsthand the price of sacrifice. He also knows the price of free will. He allowed it to happen. He knew it from the beginning of time and still chose to do it. He knows people will quit believing in Him. He knows they will cry out and scream and beg. He not only knows, but He also knew it from the beginning. And He chose to give us free will anyway. God made the willful decision to give us free will at all cost.

Has anyone ever taken the time to think of this from God's perspective? Seriously. A God who cares so much about us that He is willing to take on the brunt of everyone's pain and suffering and answers with patience and kindness and love?

The truth is that we all die. So why not live a life that honors those who sacrificed everything? A life in which we can make a profound impact in this world. All with our choices based on free will.

And yet, even knowing this, in the end it sometimes feels as if it is not enough. Why? Because in the time when we are hurting the worst, begging God not to let our loved ones die, they do. We revert back to wanting what we want, period. We want a different outcome. And where is God in the midst of death and our grief afterward? He sits on His throne.

But He is not uncaring or complacent. He waits to jump up and run toward us just like the father whose son took his inheritance and squandered it all. The father still ran to his son when he saw him coming from a long way away. And in the same way, God will run and shout to you as well, "My son, I love you. It will all be okay. I've got this." For this is not the end. This is just the beginning. The beginning of eternity. This will forever impact what you do and see, and how you will live – forever.

And yet, all we can see is but 70 years of it all,[41] 70 years in which we sometimes experience pain and suffering, life and death, joy and celebration and everything in between. But we blame God for not doing what we want Him to do. And yet death is part of it all. Death is the transition into eternal life. We cannot get to eternity without shedding mortality. And yet we fight it as if it's the last thing we will ever experience. It's like watching a baby try desperately not to fall asleep; although, in the end, sleep overtakes the little one to provide what is needed in order to move on to the

---

[41] The only thing we see with any clarity, though, is that which lies behind us. The future remains unclear, so we do the best we can based on our belief system (remember those voices inside us). Hence the need to endorse the belief system of a God who not only sees it all but also created it all.

next day. But still babies fight it. It is a losing battle, but one they are not willing to give up easily. It is no different with us and death.

In reality, eternity and heaven are the beginning of something we cannot even fathom. God can see it. He can see it as clearly as anything in the world. He created it. Utter beauty and serenity. But we fight it with all we have. And why do we do this? Because we truly do not have God's perspective. For if we did, we would gladly usher in an eschatological perspective.

And so it goes that we have no choice but to live by faith. We have to. We are not God. We have not seen it. We sometimes do not believe, and we say it isn't true, but God knows. He knows it all. He can see it. But we are mere mortals, and we have trouble believing. Believing and seeing and understanding. But what if... what if we actually had God's eyes? His perspective? His vantage point? How would we then live?

THERAPEUTIC INTERVENTION

When I do therapy, there is one particular task that I have found very helpful in gaining an eschatological perspective. I start by asking people to give me a timeline for what happened. I ask for specifics about how their friend got killed or whatever the trauma entailed. Getting facts to start them talking helps, and then I begin the process of asking for vivid details. Do not merely answer the questions I ask below in your head. Instead, actually write out the answers. You will use all the information from the questions below, so keep this information readily available as you work through the events that unfolded.

1. Can you tell me what year this happened? _____

2. What was your buddy's name who was killed (or traumatic event)? _____

3. So, they've been dead for a total of how many years? _____

4. In what capacity did you know each other?

_____

_____

5. I know this can be difficult to think about, even write about, but you are doing great. Keep thinking, keep writing. In remembering what happened, combat veterans can remember what occurred as if it happened yesterday. They can visualize it as if they are watching a movie in high definition. Let's continue. On the day it happened, I wasn't there, so help me see it from your perspective. Tell me how the day started and what was happening that led up to it. Then share with me, as best you can, the events as they unfolded, in detail, such as the terrain, the vehicles, the number of people involved, the sounds, the smells. Relive the story, but take me on the journey with you so I can better understand what you went through. The next few pages will be about writing out the account. I know it's difficult to do this work. No one said this would be easy. But it definitely has the potential to help!

The account of what happened from MY perspective:

_____

_____

_____

_____

_____

_____

_____

_____

_____

_____

_____

_____

_____

_____

_____

_____

Now that you have written out your account of what happened, and I hope it wasn't an impossible task, I have a few questions I'd like to ask.

Intervention

1. Q: I'm not sure if you consider yourself a spiritual person or not, but where do you believe your buddy is right now?

   _____

   A: Most will say in heaven.

2. So _____ (buddy's first name) has been in heaven since _____ (enter the year from above), correct?

3. How would you describe what heaven looks like to you?

_____

_____

4. And you've been living in hell since _____ (enter year as above), is that correct?

5. So, _____ (buddy's first name) has been living in heaven for _____ years, and you've been living in hell for _____ years, correct?

6. Describe what hell on earth has been like for you.

_____

_____

_____

_____

_____

_____

So, all this time, _____ (buddy's first name) has been enjoying God's perfection in heaven, and you, well, you've literally been having to endure hell on earth. You know _____ (buddy's first name) far better than I do; what do you think s/he would say to you right now?

_____

_____

_____

_____

Tell me more. What else would they say?

_____

_____

_____

_____

Is there anything else you can think of they would say?

_____

_____

_____

_____

7. Let's talk about what we do know. Sometimes people wonder why God let them live and others die. I have no idea because I don't know the mind of God. Neither do you. But what we do know is this:

   a. First, _____ (buddy's first name) is in heaven.

   b. Second, you have been living hell on earth.

   c. Third, _____ (buddy' first name) would tell you (repeat what you wrote about what his buddy would tell him):

   _____

   _____

   _____

   _____

8. How does it sound when I repeat that all back to you?

My challenge to you:

One of the very best ways we can honor those who have died is to live a life that would honor their memory, make them proud and never let them be forgotten. I can think of nothing worse than to have their death be irrelevant. Clearly, they made an impact on this earth. Just look at the impact they have made in your life!

I believe that your buddy wouldn't want you to live hell on earth either. As a matter of fact, we all raised our hands to serve this country, to be willing to sacrifice our life, if that is what it took, for freedom, and safety, and for us to live without fear. They made the ultimate sacrifice and did so freely. We all raised our hands "to protect and defend the Constitution of the United States against enemies both foreign and domestic." They fulfilled their mission and commitment to our great nation.

They are in heaven just waiting for the day that we get there. But honestly, it's not our time yet. I don't know why or when it will be our time, but our mission continues, and we cannot fail. We not only have a mission, but we also have to have a purpose and a hope and a future. Their mission is complete, and ours, well, ours is still before us, but in the end, we will all be together again, that is for certain. Their death was not in vain unless we let that happen. And we will not let that happen! We can honor their memory by how we live our lives and by what we do now and in the future.

I believe they would want us to honor them by doing everything we can to live our life in a matter worthy of such sacrifice. Living in hell, beating ourselves up, dying slowly, is not honoring them. Instead, we need to figure out what God would call us to do with whatever time we have left and run the race marked out for us. We have no choice but to press on, to take care of our family first, and that includes our brothers and sisters who are hurting and can't see they, too, are slowly dying. We have to stop this ridiculous suicide rate of people killing themselves. We are trained to kill others, not ourselves!

We need to see this not just from our perspective, but from God's perspective. He allowed them to enter heaven, our ultimate home. They may have come home way too early for *us*, but they are home and living in heaven. That is beyond anything we can even imagine. They are more than fine. As a matter of fact, I bet they would say, "Just wait until you see this place. I can't even describe it. There are simply no words that will do it justice!"

I wonder how life would change if you would consider saying the following?

"I, _____ (state your name), have an opportunity to impact this world because of what I have seen, and I know how precious life is. I need to stop looking at this from just my vantage point; I need to see this from God's perspective. God is taking care of _____ (your buddy's first name). He's not only being taken care of, but he's also living the ultimate dream. We talk about living the dream; he's actually doing it. My time on earth is not finished. There is much more to do. I only get one shot at life, and I already know how short it can be. I've seen too many lives cut short. There is no time to lose. I cannot live in hell on earth and do what God wants me to do."

NO! It's our time. We were left to carry on for such a time as this.

I have no idea what God has planned for you. You may not know either, but one thing is certain. We have a mission. Not only are our friends dying, but they have also bought into the lies. We need to fix our eyes on God and ask, "What do you want me to do?" "Where do you want me to go?"

Remember, Isaiah said it best, "Here I am Lord, send me."

We need an Army (or Navy or Air Force or Marines) of people who can see things from God's perspective. We can no longer afford to live the way we are living. The stakes are simply too high. We are on a mission, and God is the commander. Our job is to be FAT: Faithful, Available, and Teachable. We need FAT people.

Are you ready to take on this mission? Are you FAT? Can you see it from God's perspective? Are you in?

One of the things I love about God is that when He sets standards, He does not deviate or change. For example, heaven is and always will be perfect. There can be no sin that resides in heaven. In fact, one of the more interesting things that I teach is that anything apart from perfection is sin. Literally, it is missing the mark as we read about in Chapter 6. God has His perfect standards as a requirement, and anything that misses the mark of perfection is disqualified. Remember, He set the rules in motion, not me. It is no wonder then that there was found only one person who was without sin and able to unroll the scrolls in the book of Revelation, and that person is not, nor ever will be, me. And I'm betting it's not you either.

Sometimes I wonder why it is, given that God can see the end state and knows the sins we will commit, that He doesn't just stop the madness and bring us all to accountability. We've already discussed his patience is due to His wanting all to be saved. I believe there could possibly be another answer to that question. If God cut short the time, some of us would argue our case against him. We would say, "I would never have done that." Yeah, you know people like that. So, He allows it, and it's hard to argue with reality.

I hope through this book, the beliefs you hold are flexible. Otherwise, if you happen to be a person who is rigidly set in your ways, the flexibility of your brain when it comes to beliefs may make this quite challenging. But again, the good news is that you get to decide.

I'm wondering if you, too, struggle in this arena. Are you so entrenched in the way you are seeing what happened that despite contrary evidence you still argue your vantage point?

On a positive note, it could simply be that you are experiencing what is called a "blind spot." It's like in your car, that spot where you just can't see the driver in the next lane, even in your rear-view mirror or your side mirror. That's when someone honks because you unknowingly pulled into the other lane because you just couldn't see that someone was there.

The good news is that we all have blind spots. But what we don't want is for people to argue that they are not there. Oh, they're there all right. And dealing with the truth of it can be quite difficult. That is why therapists will say that the first step to getting help and getting better is to acknowledge the problem.

And remember, because of human nature, we will always find arguments for our case. We can always make an argument for why we don't want to change or do things differently. The problem here is that the arguments only entrench us deeper into our "perspective," which is keeping us stuck. We have to be willing to see things from a different perspective, possibly even from God's perspective, in order to get out of our situation.

Why is this important? Because as humans, we like to argue. We are our own worst enemy. And no one can lie to ourselves better than we can. You see, we are convinced that it is our fault. It's our fault the person died. If only we had... and then the entrenchment happens. We make arguments repeatedly about why it is our fault that something happened. And the reality is there is often a bit of truth in them; otherwise, we wouldn't accept them. But are we to blame for our friend getting killed because of what we did or did not do? Many will argue yes, and the entrenchment only continues.

THE BURDEN OF BLAME

What I will often do is ask veterans to assign a percentage of blame. I will ask, "How much do you blame yourself for your buddy's death?" The person may respond "100%." Then I ask, "Do you put any blame on the person who sent you there?" and they will say, "Okay, maybe 90%, and 10% was our leadership. But I'm still 90% to blame!" and the entrenchment continues.

Then I'll press a bit harder. "Did you shoot them?" They will respond, "Of course not." Then I'll ask, "Who did?" and they will often say an insurgent. Then I'll ask whether the insurgent is at fault in any way. What percentage of blame will you give them? Zero?

Over time, these veterans will begin to shift their percentages and perspectives about who is 100 percent at fault, starting with their being 100% at fault and now possibly being 50-75% at fault. It is the beginning of the truth we are after. Inevitably, they will say, "But if I had only.... then maybe they would still be alive." The issue here is that one is arguing for an unknown. We simply do not know what would have happened because the circumstances did not play out that way.

Starting from the end state and working our way backward, we are left with the questions most people start with. And most start with "What if."

- "What if I had only...."
- "What if we had taken a different route?"
- "What if I had gone first instead of them?"
- "What if command had not made us go on that convoy, at least that day?"
- "What if we had not stopped the convoy?"
- "What if I had just...."

In trying to make sense of it all, or even wishing we could have had a different outcome, we play the "What if?" game. Unfortunately, we may not know the answer to that question until we see God face to face and we ask. Then, and only then, may we get our final answer. Until then, what will you do? Continue to look at the shattered pieces at your feet? Or will you make a willful decision to see things from God's perspective and become your own artist and create your own ending to the story?

You see, it is still true. God has given us free will. We get to choose.

What will you do?

CHAPTER 13: THE MISSION CONTINUES

Gaining an eschatological (big picture, eternal) perspective will undoubtedly change your life. It will change not only how you see the world, others and yourself, but it will also have a direct impact on your choices and your behavior. Although I have tried to lay out an eschatological perspective on trauma, it is an incredibly significant but not completely sufficient answer. In this final chapter, I would like to introduce you to one final perspective that I believe, although difficult to grasp, will have just as much impact on your life. We have heard many times "we've got your six" in the military. This chapter is not only about who has your back but also about who has your front and your sides as well.

MOVING FORWARD

What I am proposing for you is the impact of Phileo. Trying to explain this concept fails in the English language for many reasons, the least of which there is simply only one word for love – love. In Greek, there are at least four.[42] For the sake of time, this chapter

---

[42] Agape (ἀγάπη *agápē*[1]), Eros (ἔρως *érōs*), Storge (στοργή *storgē*) and Phileo (φιλία *philía*).

will focus on Phileo, brotherly love. Philadelphia, the city of "brotherly love," has its root meaning in this word and is an easy way to remember it.

I define Phileo as something beyond, "I've got your back." It is a sacrifice and service that will stop at nothing to accomplish its mission. Nothing. When a brother is hurting, you intervene. When somebody's life is on the line, you are the one who is willing to sacrifice. Combine this with Agape, an unconditional love, and you've got one's back, front, sides, their whole body, mind and soul.

It is a love that is an intensely close bond, similar to what we had in the military when people had our six. There was no question whether our brothers and sisters in arms would do everything within their power to watch out for us and keep us alive. As a matter of fact, you know as well as I do that there are only a few people in this world who would go to such lengths, most of whom are in the "less than one percenters" category. Only a few in this world would willingly take a bullet, dive on a grenade, or take lead on a potentially deadly mission. It is this selfless sacrifice that few will ever know, a sacrifice so intense, that when others make it, it makes us feel as if we are unworthy to even be alive.

Some of you have literally been on the receiving end of such selfless sacrifice. Some of you are alive today because of other's actions. You may even suffer from survivor guilt because of it. Why? Because a buddy stood in the gap and made the ultimate sacrifice.

When we are on the receiving end of such sacrifice, there is an overwhelming conflictual feeling of appreciation and thankfulness but also a feeling of guilt and feelings of unworthiness. We simply feel as if we do not deserve to be alive. We feel as if we do not deserve what we have been given. To be on the receiving end of such sacrifice, such giving, such willingness to lay one's life down for ours, is simply too much. We feel unworthy to receive what is called "unmerited favor." We didn't do anything to earn it. It was simply given out of pure sacrifice.

If there was a choice given, we would have been the one to volunteer. We would gladly risk our lives for those around us. We would gladly trade places. But sometimes, there are limited options, and the choice of sacrifice by others was made. To be honest, it's the acceptance of such sacrifice that is at the root of survivor guilt.

Let's talk about what it's like to be on the receiving end of such actions. For someone to sacrifice their life for ours is unfathomable. When we do have time to contemplate such actions and ponder such sacrifice, it leads to feeling as if we have been given a payment for a debt we could never repay. There is no way to reciprocate. We would if we could, but we cannot.

It is this sacrifice, this overwhelming gift that we have personally experienced, but trying to articulate such a gift is a difficult task. Let us attempt such a challenge by putting it into a military, judicial context.

SCENE 1: MAI LAI

The date: March 16, 1968. Joe was a first sergeant in Charlie Company in Vietnam. They had received intelligence that the Viet Cong (VC) had taken refuge in Quang Ngai village of Son My. Imagine you are Joe. As a platoon, you are on a search and destroy mission. But instead of finding VC guerillas, you find unarmed old men, women and children. The soldiers had been advised before the attack that anyone found in the city could be considered VC or VC sympathizers, and they were told to destroy the village. According to History.com, "They acted with extraordinary brutality, raping and torturing villagers before killing them and dragging dozens of people, including young children and babies, into a ditch and executing them with automatic weapons. The massacre reportedly ended when an Army helicopter pilot, Warrant Officer Hugh Thompson, landed his aircraft between the soldiers and the retreating villagers and threatened to open fire if they continued their attacks." Over 500 people were killed that day.

High ranking military officers attempted to cover it up, but God makes it clear, that which is done in secret will be revealed. And in this case, it made international news.

Although an incredibly difficult scenario to be forced into, there were some who did exactly what they were told. They followed orders. And in this scenario, it is you who followed orders.

Years later, there is a trial in which you and others must stand and be tried. And what is your defense? "I was following orders," you reply while under oath. The problem: you killed innocent people. An armed man with the power, authority and weapons to take life, and you did.

Weeks and weeks of testimony have been gathered. The sequestered jury has taken all day to deliberate your outcome. A decision has been made.

"Will the defendant please rise" is pronounced as you have awaited this dreadful day.

The judge, a widely respected three-star general, had been called on to oversee the process. Deep down inside you know that following orders in the military is what we do, but you also know that killing innocent people, including women and children, is not what we do. You've gone over the situation in your head many times. Replayed it over and over, making arguments within yourself on both sides. But in the end, you know. You know you shouldn't have done it. You know it wasn't the right thing to do. Blame it on anger, blame it on revenge, blame it on an order, blame it on whatever you can concoct in your head, but when you lay down to rest and put your head on your pillow at night, you know it was you who pulled the trigger. You see their faces. It was you who killed innocent people. It was you who will stand before God and be held accountable. There is no one to blame but yourself. You had a choice, you had free will, and you used it. This is how you seem to lose track of time. So many thoughts are in your head while the world around you keeps moving forward, but to you, time stands still. As you blink repeatedly and try to come back to what is in front of you, you take one last deep breath. And then the verdict.

The judge goes over the case, giving a synopsis of the events as they transpired, reading details of that day which are incredibly hard to hear, let alone fathom. Is it really you who did this? Did that really happen? It's like it's a totally different person. Someone other than yourself. No wonder people feel is if they are no longer themselves when they experience such flashbacks of strong memories. You can still smell the rapid fire of automatic weapons going off around you and the hot bullet casings ejecting right next to you.

Methodically, the judge gives specifics of the situation, what you are being accused of, and the evidence that convicts you. The jurors have come to a unanimous decision.

The judge looks at you straight in the eye as the verdict is read by the lead juror: "We, the jury, find the defendant guilty of murder as charged in the indictment."

Your shoulders and whole body sink down into the earth as these words are read. Your head drops as the juror continues, "We, the jury, recommend that the defendant be punished by death. The vote is as follows: 12 for death, zero for life without parole."

As you stand there in total silence, you can feel your chest rise and fall. You flashback and relive what had transpired on that horrible day. There are other legal options, but you know deep down inside that you have no defense. There is nothing left. You did what they said you did. There is no escaping justice. An eye for an eye. A life for a life. In this case, death for death.

What would you do if you were in that position, at that moment, knowing what you know and knowing what you did? Justice will be served. It is simply down to you, this judge and imminent death.

What hope is there? Is there any answer at all? When your back is against the wall, is there anyone who will come to your rescue?

The reason this book was written is because I believe there is. There is an answer because I have experienced it. An answer that is so solid, it's like a rock. Maybe you've been there, maybe not to the extent of this example, but where we no longer have a defense, we no longer have hope. We no longer feel as if we are worthy. We have participated in such egregious acts in our lives that we know, beyond a shadow of doubt, if there is a heaven, we won't be there. We are unworthy of acceptance, unworthy of entrance. And because of such acts of transgression, we are brought to our knees because we are truly being honest about who we are and what we have done. We know that we cannot solve this problem ourselves.

That moment is the turning point, the point where decisions are made. Many feel hopeless and see no way out. They are beyond bottomless. There is simply no escaping one's self and what we are capable of and what we have done.

It wasn't but a few years ago that you decided to raise your hand and join the military. To be willing to sacrifice your life if called upon. To be willing to lay down your life for others. To write a check for your life that could be cashed at any moment's notice. What you didn't do was join the military to kill innocent people, especially women and children. That, in your opinion, is dishonorable, and the opposite of your intent.

You may have joined the military, just like in this scenario, because your father was in the military. Maybe you see your dad as an honorable man, a man you wanted to emulate, a man whom you believe always did the right thing - in this case, an amazing lawyer whom you called on for help, but he chose not to respond. Your pleas for help seemed to fall on deaf ears. No response, nothing. Just like God when he remained silent, so, too, your dad says nothing.

Feeling ashamed and alone in this world, you have never felt like this in your life. You figure he was too embarrassed, dishonored and unwilling to even acknowledge you as his son. So you stand, about to be court-martialed as a man convicted of wrongdoing and one that is about to die.

SCENE 2: THE REVELATION

And then it happens.

The judge does something nobody expects.

Totally out of character and totally out of nowhere, you see the judge begin peeling off a mask that has been created to hide one's true self, a skin that has been designed at DARPA[43] to mimic a human face that is undetectable. Clearly, they had been successful. As he peels off the neoprene-like skin, everyone in the courtroom is confused but watches quietly, intently. Bit by bit, he takes off the remaining pieces of flesh like material which reveals his true self.

Astounded by what you see, it is like a scene out of Star Wars when Darth Vader reveals that he is Luke Skywalker's father (spoiler alert). Only in this case, this three-star general and judge who has presided over the case is none other than your father.

He looks straight at you and does not blink. While you were sacrificing your life on the battlefield, he was stateside serving our country as a military judge. He has seen enough, heard enough, and

---

[43] Defense Advanced Research Projects Agency

says so, "ENOUGH. I have seen and heard enough. God has brought me to this point in my career and in my life for such a time as this. You are my son whom I dearly love. I will serve in your place. The sacrifice of death, I will pay it."

Totally surprised, shocked and confused, you and everyone around you look at each other. And by a strange set of events, including military justice and military law that sometimes doesn't make sense, *he has such authority*. Believe it or not, the jurors only recommend, it is the judge who decides. His decision is final and irrevocable. And his final decision: "I will serve in your place." A father who loves his son so much he would be willing to convict you but also die for you. Justice must be served, and a price will be paid. But instead of you being the one to pay, he makes the decision that it will be him.

Can this really happen? Can legally this even be possible? Although there would be a conflict of interest in the judge hearing the case (which would be one argument against it), don't miss the point. Justice must be served, and someone will pay it. But in this case, it's that same, "I've got your back" response, only this time it hits close to home. It is from your dad. So, let me ask you this. If this scenario would even be possible, how would you feel if this did truly happen?

Seriously, contemplate it for a few moments. What would you think about such sacrifice? Especially from your own dad. What emotions would be going through you at the time? What would you think about his substituting himself in your place? It's called substitutionary atonement. It's when you are replaced by someone who bears the brunt of what you should receive.

Would you feel unworthy? Would you be the first to argue against it? Would you try to stop it?

Personally, once I understood the magnitude of such actions, I would object. I would object to my father taking my place. I

150

wouldn't allow it. And yet the problem is exactly the same problem we have when someone next to us gets killed. We object. We want a different outcome. We want to either change the scenario or be the one who sacrifices. There is something about the American military member where we are willing to live and die for our country. But we don't do well when it's those next to us who give up their lives for us. The problem? We don't get to decide. These decisions are out of our control and not something we have the power to decide. Reality dictates. And in our story, it's the father who has the authority, not us. And with God, He has the authority, not us.

Instead, we have to accept reality. And the reality is that once we lose someone to death, our life and our mission continues. Even if we chose not to decide, that is a choice. In situations of survivor guilt and moral injury, one thing remains: the person struggles with feelings of unworthiness. The real question shifts from why this happened to what will happen. What will you do with this gift of life, the remainder of your time on earth?

You see, it is precisely this gift that I have received on a personal, intimate basis that drives me to serve others. We have been given grace beyond anything we could ever ask or imagine. It is not just our fathers who have sacrificed for our well-being; it is God himself. He was willing to allow His Son to pay the ultimate price for sin so that we can be forgiven. There will be no sermon here. We are just overwhelmed by the experience of such sacrifice made on our behalf.

But just as we spent significant amounts of time in this book trying to see things from an eschatological perspective, one thing we do know for certain. One day we will stand before God and give account for what we did with the time we were given. Imagine the scenario with us.

SCENE 3: JUDGMENT DAY

Satan himself, the accuser, knowing all that you have done in your life, decides personally to argue his case against you for all you have said and done. Every egregious act, every sin, everything you thought was hidden, he reveals. Things you never wanted anyone to know. Things you wanted to bury and pray never came up. One accusation after another and deep down inside, just like with Mai Lai, you know it's true. There is no escaping it. It all happened just as Satan describes. He is, of course, described as the accuser for a reason.

After his diatribe of repeated accusatory truths, Satan delivers the final blow. He turns to God and says, "How, how could you let someone like this into perfection? He is the exact opposite of perfection. Look at what he has done and who he has hurt. Look at all of this evidence!"

Satan then points directly at God and says, "And remember, God, you made the rules. It is you who set them up, and they cannot be broken. It only takes one sin. Just one. And this man is full of sin. Everywhere he turns, he sins. This is an open and shut case!"

As you look into God's eyes, tears fall until you are completely broken. You fall to your knees in complete surrender because you know the truth. There is no defense. There is nothing you can say. Nothing you can do. Everything is true. Everything.

And where is God? Listening, watching, sitting on His throne.

You know deep down inside that God can do anything he wants. But what will he do in your case? Everything that has been said is true, and you are not worthy of heaven. He will not go against his own rules. He is God after all. And in truth, you not only have one sin, you have a multitude of sins. And because heaven is perfect, nothing imperfect can reside there. That same deep sigh of complete and total acceptance of one's reality is expelled in your breath as it escapes your body. Complete surrender.

SCENF 4: THE BOOK

So, what does God do at a time like this? We have no idea. We've never been in such a situation. No one has that can tell us. What we do know is that there are none who are worthy. It even says that there are scrolls that are to be unrolled, but they cannot be unrolled by anyone who has sin. It would be like trying to earn your way into heaven by being able to throw a quarter across the Grand Canyon. No matter how good you are or strong you think you might be, your attempts will fall incredibly short, so short, it's not even worth attempting. So now what? Where is the hope we so desperately need?

This same God who sits on his throne, turns and picks up the Lamb's Book of Life. And in this massive book, He begins to flip through the pages methodically, one page at a time. You hear the ruffling of pages, one after the other.

God knows the exact page, but He does it in front of Satan, just to remind him who is in charge. You see, your name matters, and you matter to God. But in this book, it's not what you have done or not done. It's about something much more important, a bigger sacrifice than you and I could ever make - a sacrifice that cost a man his life.

This is the only book where your name counts more than anywhere else in the world. As God flips the pages, He gets toward the end of the book and points precisely with an emphatic gesture. He looks up from the book and with a clear and definitive voice says your full name out loud while you stand there.

God turns to you and says, "This is your name, is it not?" as he smiles in victory over such accusations. "Yes, yes, it is," as you humbly and tearfully in brokenness and thankfulness respond. The price of forgiveness has been paid in blood.

God turns to Satan, "His name is right here, written in the Lamb's Book of Life. His sins have been covered. The price has been paid. I see no sin in him."

And then God stands. He opens up his arms and gives you the biggest hug you could ever imagine and says to you, "Enter into my kingdom, good and faithful servant."

You melt in His arms, and there is nothing left to be said. Tears fall as He holds the weight of your body. God's not only got your back; He's got all of you. And Satan? Satan angrily walks away. He's lost another battle. A battle for the human soul.

Can you imagine it? Can you even fathom such an experience? Personally, it would be overwhelming. What clearly matters is that your name is written and, more precisely, written in this book that impacts eternity![44]

In this book where I have emphasized an eschatological approach to healing, can you imagine how your life would change if you saw the world from this perspective? Can you imagine how it would impact your life? Your decisions? Your behavior? Your worth? Your hope? Your future?

You see, this is how God is at work. He knows about sacrifice to the point of death. He is, after all, not only the giver of life but also the one who has authority over death. He was willing to allow his own son to die for this very reason. And when one grasps that reality, it completely changes everything.

In Romans 6, when pondering such incredible sacrifice, the question came up, "Shall we sin even more so that the sacrifice is

---

[44] If you don't know whether your name is written in the Lamb's Book of Life or not, please contact a spiritual advisor that you trust and deem to be knowledgeable.

even greater?" By no means. Instead, it should compel us to be thankful even now for what we have been given. To know that when we ask God's forgiveness, it is freely given. But do not mistake freedom for free. It came at a significant sacrifice, just like the sacrifice we make in the military. We know freedom isn't free. And this freedom from sin is no different. It had to be paid with a price. And, thank God, it has already been paid.

It is this free gift of life and freedom in Him that compels us to the work that we do at Project Healing Heroes. You see, we actually believe there are real answers for real problems, not just, "tell us how you feel." We are driven, and the mission continues because of what we have been given. Our prayer is that you, too, will be able to see things from an eschatological perspective. It is, after all, our mission to give people a hope and a future.

"For I know the plans I have for you," declares the Lord, "plans to prosper you and not to harm you, plans to give you hope and a future." (Jeremiah 29:11)

APPENDIX: CONFRONTING THE ELEPHANT - SUICIDE

Statistically, there are roughly 1 million people who die by suicide each year.[45] According to the Department of Veterans Affairs, 20 veterans die from suicide each day. This begs the question of - why are so many people killing themselves? Unless you have personally been through the stronghold of despair and depression, it's difficult to comprehend, let alone grasp. There are many reasons why people may suicide, one of which may be that people are in so much pain they can see no other way out. They believe their options have been depleted. **Suicide is their final decision to escape unbearable suffering.**

The answers to the depths of suicide are beyond the scope of this book. However, I would like to provide a list of resources and answers to questions that people often have about suicide, whether it be for themselves or someone they care about.

When people are hurting, please remember that an individualized response is obviously the most helpful. Each person is unique in his or her life circumstances and can no longer see a way out. If professional help is available, we highly highly recommend you connect such help to that person as soon as

---

[45] https://www.helpguide.org/articles/suicide-prevention/suicide-prevention.htm

possible. In the meantime, here are my top 25 suggestions to consider:

1. **The US national suicide hotline number is 1-800-273-TALK (8255).** To find a suicide helpline outside the US, visit the International Association for Suicide Prevention (IASP) or Suicide.org.

2. **Never leave the person alone.** Ever. Once you suspect a person is suicidal, do whatever is necessary to keep that person within your direct line of sight. If nothing else, it shows you care.

3. **Ask the obvious.** It is a myth that if you ask if a person who is suicidal the question, this will create what is called, "thought insertion" where the person now becomes suicidal. People actually find relief that someone is attuned to their world and struggles that they care enough to ask.

4. **Actions speak louder than words.** If the person says he or she is not suicidal but is giving away personal items, doesn't have future orientation, appears depressed, and other types of behavior correlated to suicide, look at that person's behavior rather than that person's words.

5. **Remove all weapons, alcohol, drugs, etc.** People who are impulsive can end up with a permanent solution to a temporary problem.

6. **People in serious acute pain are at increased risk for suicide.** Try to get them to a pain specialist or the Emergency Department ASAP. If they are drug seeking, that is for the expert to decide.

7. **Consider a wellness check.** If you have someone who is suicidal on the telephone, alert someone to call police and request a wellness check. If nothing else, a wellness check shows you care.

8. **People that are suicidal may not say anything.** They want out of pain whether that be emotional or physical pain. They may not say anything because they simply no longer want to be a burden to others.

9. **They won't do it, because they talk about it all the time.** People who threaten repeatedly may be attention seeking. Whether intentionally or on accident, suicide can and does occur.

10. **They are feeling better so they must be ok.** People are actually more susceptible to suicide when they start getting energy back. The reason is that they may have been so depressed that when they do have energy, they realize how miserable they are and thus have the energy to act.

11. **Anniversary and "Alive" dates.** If a person survived when others got killed, you could see how this would be a difficult time. Do your best to be proactive, especially at times when you know people struggle.

12. **Suicide contracts will stop them.** These have statistically not been all that helpful. What has been more helpful is a strong relationship and a promise to you that they will give you a chance to talk in person before they do anything. Make them promise you that they won't do anything until you at least have the chance to be with them, not just an attempt to contact. People have a hard time breaking promises to people they care about. Others won't make that promise, and that should alert you to the seriousness of the situation.

13. **Alcohol and drug use reduces inhibition.** People are not always rational at times under the influence. Keep this in mind, and alert help (police, suicide hotline, etc.) immediately, and keep them on the phone or in line of site at all times.

14. **Circumstances in life are temporary.** Not all, but most. If you can, with integrity, be there for them, tell them.

15. **Don't make promises you can't keep.** People know when they are being lied to. If a person is in stage 4 cancer, don't promise them that they can beat it. You don't know any better than they do about their future. Promise them what you can control: your actions and your willingness to be there with them through it.

16. **Sleep.** Sometimes people who are suicidal just need sleep. When appropriate, hold them and help create a relaxed atmosphere. If they are in an atmosphere that is causing problems, take them somewhere else. Reduce noise, distractions, triggers.

17. **Medications.** If they are used to taking medications, get it for them. Don't let them get it themselves. Or, if they refuse, watch them. And if they get angry, tell them it's because you care too much to not intervene. You suspect they would do the same for you and make that the issue.

18. **Role reversal.** Ask them what they would do for you if you were in their situation (assuming they can think rationally and clearly). Sometimes their answer may surprise you and give you insight into what they would really like for you to do for them.

19. **Don't go it alone.** Get others involved as appropriately as possible, but do not attempt to do this in isolation.

20. **Ask permission.** It's always best to ask people for permission before you do something, but if they refuse, you don't have to follow what they say. But if they give permission, it makes things easier.

21. **Help them think about it from the perspective of people who love and care for them.** If they have children, talk about how devastated they would be growing up without a

father, for example. Use their first names, and make it personal.

22. **Talk about their successes (if appropriate)**. Acknowledge the difficulty they have been through, but also remind them of their successes. Try to think of things they cannot argue with you about.

23. **Death by cop.** Sometimes, people feel that suicide is not an option. Therefore, if they die by another person's hands, that is a different story. In the rare circumstance that you are present in this type of situation, tell the police, "He is trying to provoke you to shoot him." Depending on his actions, the authorities will have to respond accordingly.

24. **Ministry of Presence.** Just sit with people, and show them by your actions that you care, especially when some people are looking for a fight. Sometimes, no matter what you say, they will argue against it. Don't give them any fuel for their anger. Don't get into religious arguments. As a matter of fact, try not to get into any arguments. It's hard to argue with someone who won't argue and cares with their actions.

25. **Intent to kill.** Even with people who are determined to die, it is a myth that you can't stop them. Research shows that people who attempted suicide and actually lived, regretted their decision. There are instances where people have jumped off buildings and then lived, regretting it on the way down.

I hope this encourages you to not question whether or not you should intervene. Please do! Their life depends on it. You may not know exactly what to say or how to say it, but it's hard to argue with someone who cares enough to act.

Remember: Suicide is a permanent solution to a temporary problem.

Made in the USA
Middletown, DE
10 May 2022